THE

PLOWMAN

SHALL OVERTAKE

THE

REAPER

ENDORSEMENTS

Lora has done it again! Her latest book is a riveting read. These pages will stir you about the coming global harvest of millions of souls into the Kingdom of God. You will learn how to be a 'reaper' in this harvest. Too often in history when the harvest is ripe, the laborers, i.e., the reapers, are few. The author challenges our faith to believe that there will be plenty of reapers for the coming plenteous harvest!

I love it when Lora points out that the harvest has both a strategy and a song! This is the way the Lord God moves forward in history. He releases strategies for the advancement of His Kingdom, and He gives His people sounds and songs from heaven so that the earth can be reaped for His glory. Indeed, the earth is the Lord's, and the harvest is His! Use this Bible filled and comprehensive manual to become equipped in your calling as a harvest-reaper. Also use it to teach others.

Jim Hodges, Founder and President
Federation of Ministers and Churches, International

The Plowman Shall Overtake The Reaper is full of prophetic metaphor, with strong symbolism from Jesus' parables and other scriptures, but the more I read, the more I realized her book was not only prophetic with a futuristic focus, but germane for today…we need the message she shares as we move forward in our Kingdom of God assignments.

I encourage you to read this dynamic work with an open heart. It is not a light read; it will take some work to get the meat being presented, but it is well worth the effort, for contained in these pages is greater illumination into the purpose of God for this generation.

Dr. Stan E. DeKoven, President
Vision International University

WOW! What a phenomenal read! *The Plowman Shall Overtake The Reaper* by Prophet Lora Allison is a priceless and inspirational work that is truly extraordinary and LIFE-CHANGING! Why didn't we put all this together long ago? This teaching is a stunning way to understand the work that the Lord is doing in our lives – in becoming whole and healed.

Dr. Kluane Spake, Apostle
http://kluane.com
dr.Kluane@kluane.com

Profound! Lora Allison has done an epic job. From the introduction to the conclusion, there are layers upon layers of insightful and needful revelations to help us understand the part we play as the greatest outpouring of God's Spirit literally bursts upon the world's stage. This book instills a hunger to be read repeatedly while being filled with revelatory passion to partner with Him, The Lord of the Harvest. Behold the days are HERE when *The Plowman Shall Overtake The Reaper*!

Jill Mitchell O'Brien, President
Kingdom Connections International, Inc.

THE

PLOWMAN

SHALL OVERTAKE

THE

REAPER

BY LORA ALLISON

COPYRIGHT

CONTENTS

FOREWORD

by Dr. Chuck D. Pierce

Behold, the days are coming," says the Lord, "When the plowman shall overtake the reaper, and the treader of grapes him who sows seed; the mountains shall drip with sweet wine, and all the hills shall flow with it. Amos 9:13 NKJV

One of the key passages to understand today is Amos 9. This chapter is critical to our future. David created a prototype that had never been seen on the earth. Under the Law, David's Tabernacle was actually illegal, but God gave the prototype! The Lord provided a supernatural release and glory for His Ark to move from one season into its position for the next. When Amos prophesied this, he said that the Tabernacle of David would be restored. For the early church to advance in confusing times, they had to refer to Amos' prophecy. The book of Revelation is about the Tabernacle of David being restored. We are living in this time now!

Recently, I was in Houston and began to share what the Lord had shown me for the year ahead. I asked Him specifically what His word was for 2019, and He said these words to me: "**PLOW THROUGH IT!**" I shared this when Lora Allison was in the meeting. I have known Lora for several years, but I forgot that she had written about plowing.

When I finished speaking, she said, "Do you remember the book I wrote several years ago about the plowmen overtaking the reapers?" I said, "Vaguely, I remember part of it." She promptly said, "The Lord instructed me to redo that book for today!"

I grabbed the opportunity to go back through the revelation that the Lord had given her. *The Plowman Shall Overtake The Reaper* is the book for this hour! I have not read anything that better represents the decade ahead. If I could recommend one book to read other than the Bible, I would say to read this.

The Tabernacle of David represents fervent prayer and praise as it was practiced under David's oversight (see 1 Chron.16:1,4). Prayer and praise in every region are key in the Church's future, but the verse in Amos 9 that speaks to me most this year is verse 13: "The plowman shall overtake the reaper." This means that great blessings are coming quickly. As we allow God to build His plan on the earth, the greater the cycle of blessings will be in our homes, churches and regions. Prophetic seeds that have been sown and declared in your region should be plowed up! The Lord has put us into a plowing season. Most importantly, He has given us this incredible tool to equip us.

The prophetic seeds that didn't come up in one season should be declared and planted again. I see teams of plowmen being connected together. Many of us have received revelation but tried to plow alone. However, if we connect and plow together, the harvest of God in a region will be gathered. There is a specific timing we must be in if we want to reap the harvest. That's why God is speaking to His Church about this passage of scripture. This is a key time for alignment. Lora addresses not only the seed and the sower, but how we must plow together in days ahead and not sow in vain.

Lora brings great understanding to every aspect of manifesting our promise. She then moves into a prophetic exhortation on the restoration of God's Garden for the future.

Biblically, God's goal for us is harvest. We see this all the way through the Bible. God wants our barns to be filled with plenty and for our vats to overflow. He wants us to experience the fullness of His promised blessing. That's what harvest means. Harvest is what we've been working for and praying for. It's the promise that God has held out before us. The promise that we have been pressing into, and the time does come when we will receive the harvest. Harvest is not "pie in the sky by and by." Harvest is the reality of the promise coming into our experience. God not only wants us to harvest in the natural realm, but also to see a harvest of righteousness. He wants us to experience a harvest of souls. But there is a time for harvest. Psalm 1 tells us that God wants us to be like a flourishing tree that brings forth its fruit in its season. Ecclesiastes 3 tells us there is a time and a season for everything. There is a time to plant seeds, and there is also a time to reap the harvest.

We must be in God's timing. God wants us to have an abundant harvest, but if we aren't in the right time and season, we will not reap it. Too often, the Church goes out to harvest in the wrong season, and instead of getting grain, it just gets snowed on. If you're not in the right season, you won't get a harvest. That's a basic principle.

God has established many laws. One of the most familiar is the law of the harvest, which says that a person will reap what he or she sows. That's a description of how the universe operates and is like the law of gravity. If you want to have a bountiful harvest, you must first sow your seed. When you understand the law of the harvest, you are enabled to prosper. A law is really just a picture of reality. It's a description of how things work. For example, the law of gravity is a description of how objects behave on planet Earth. On this planet, when you let go of an object, it falls. That's the law of gravity.

Satan uses times and laws to stop God's people from advancing and manifesting His grace and power. Daniel 7:25 says that Satan tries to wear down our minds, or ways of thinking, to capture us and consequently capture the blessings and promises God intended for us. Once we agree or fall prey to Satan's ways, we begin to decrease rather than increase. The enemy's plan of devastation takes effect, and we begin to lose the war of resisting.

When this happens, we move from operating in the laws of prosperity and begin to embrace poverty. Satan overtakes our minds with a flood of thoughts that starts this reversal. Instead of thinking prosperity and meditating on the covenant that God has with us, we develop a poverty mindset. We must remain alert to what is happening in our field, or the enemy will attempt to get his hands on what belongs to us. When we grow passive and are not aware of the enemy's scheme to rob our supplies and assets, he maneuvers and manipulates his way into the storehouses meant for us. When the enemy gains an upper hand over our inheritance, we lose our stewardship ability to multiply. When we fail to capitalize on the opportunity to bring in our harvest, he steals the field.

We can plant, watch our crops grow and have breakthrough, but if we do not take the opportunity to gather and steward the spoils, a strategy of poverty will begin to develop against us. Remember the story of Gideon. Every year at harvest times, for seven years, the Midianites would let Israel grow the harvest and then come to steal, rob and plunder. When we increase without developing storehouses to contain our spoils, we eventually lose the spoils, and poverty begins to work.

Refusing to become what God created and destined you to be causes poverty to work in your life. Not believing that the Lord can branch you into the fullness of His plan is just as bad as refusing to become what He intended and created you to become. Poverty thinking is not just experiencing lack, but also having a fear that you will lack. When you conform to your circumstances or come into agreement with the blueprint of the world, the prince of this world will use you until he has fully captured your strength for his purpose.

THIS BOOK WAS SAVED FOR THE BODY OF CHRIST FOR NOW! Most of us do not understand harvest time. Because of our complex lives, we are far removed from the actual production of our food supplies and the source of our provision. The harvest was significant (see Gen. 8:22; 45:6). Events were reckoned from harvests (see Gen. 30:14; Josh. 3:15; Judg. 15:1; Ruth 1:22; 2:23; 1 Sam. 6:13; 2 Sam. 21:9; 23:13). For instance, take the Pentecost Feast which represents:

- A season of gathering (see Zech. 8)
- A season of judgment (see Jer. 51:33; Joel 3:13; Rev 14:15)
- A season of grace (see Jer. 8:20)
- A time for the good news to be heard (see Matt. 9:37-38; John 4:35)
- An end of a season and beginning of a new season of provision (see Mt. 13:39)

This book is for now! His Word that He gave us is built around harvest. This harvest includes both physical as well as spiritual blessings. We must know our moment. Another unction the Lord gave me for all of us was, "Tell My people not to miss their moment!" It is vital, for our future. I often sense that we are a people who miss much of what we should see. I believe the Lord is saying, "Look again!" He wants us to see beyond—to see in ways we have not seen and what He has prepared for us. To see beyond where we presently see, both spiritually and physically, we must become aware that God IS opening up our path ahead. (Psalm 21)

An important dimension of life is to see eye-to-eye with the person we are communicating with, whether in business, ministry, family, or any relationship. But most importantly we want to see eye-to-eye and face-to-face with the One who created us, who knows us best, and knows our future. God wants to give us clear VISION! This is a pressing time to see our vision clearly. Proverbs 29:18 warns us that: "Where there is no vision, the people perish" (KJV). Lack of vision will destroy our motivation, and without vision we fall into passivity and discouragement. Having a clear vision keeps us moving forward toward our goal.

I look at the Church as a Storehouse. The Lord is preparing a new storehouse for harvest. God is now unlocking and decoding seeds to provide our future. The principles of resurrection and power in the seed is important because it unlocks what needs to be brought forth.

Again, the Lord has saved this book for now. I decree that this book will go all over the world to help the plowman overtake the reaper.

Dr. Chuck D. Pierce
President, Global Spheres Inc.
President, Glory of Zion Intl.

PREFACE

"Behold, the days are coming," saith the Lord, "when the plowman shall overtake the reaper, and the treader of grapes him who sows seed; and the mountains shall drip with sweet wine, and all the hills shall flow with it.

And I will bring back the captives of My people Israel; they shall build the waste cities and inhabit them; they shall plant vineyards, and drink wine from them; they shall also make gardens and eat fruit from them.

And I will plant them in their land, and no longer shall they be pulled up from the land I have given them," says the Lord your God. Amos 9:13-15 NKJV

So many of us look forward to that wondrous event so discussed, taught about, and prophesied—the mighty end-time harvest. (Rev. 14:15-16) Often it is viewed as a time of joy, of ingathering and merriment. But we never hear much about the work that surely must be involved, as literally millions of souls are reborn into the kingdom. Where are the laborers who will go into the fields of this momentous event to plow, and plant, to water and thresh and winnow? All the time-honored events so graphically illustrated by farmers in real fields with mouths to feed and a "living" to make, all of those labors will continue in the time of the great harvest as young Christians are taught, trained and raised up.

Change is now upon the horizon, and the lessons learned from Jesus' parables of the soil and the sower must be relearned and reapplied to fit the changing season. "In that day the plowman shall overtake the reaper..." What does this mean? Where are we going as we reply, "here am I, send me"? What is our place in this strategic season of the unfolding of the ends of the ages?

The prophets are blowing trumpets, teachers are teaching, apostles are gathering, and each of the five-fold ministry is equipping and building the saints to take their place in the awesome end-time army of husbandmen sent into the fields of the world. Like the children of Israel in the wilderness, many are crying Where are we going? When will we get there? What will it be like? But comfortable or not, understood or not—the cloud is moving, the trumpet has sounded and the great mass of God's people is once again on the move.

The following somewhat radical but highly Biblical prophetic word given to the Church through Lora Allison several years ago will be explored in scripture throughout the rest of the book. So don't worry! The obscure will become clear as we view God's end-time plan!

PARABLE OF THE ARMY

"From the heart of God, there is coming a wave of living light. A glittering, shattering wave of pure, unadulterated light; a supernatural, laser-quality light so white and so bright and so hot that it will annihilate and swallow all darkness before its path, eliminating and exposing the terror and fear, the deception, the horror, the apostasy so rampant in the world. It will expose the looks upon the faces of the living dead. Even as the brilliant light of a flash bulb has that quality of shock, so will this wave of light instantly flash across the face of the earth.

Many will run from this light, trying to escape. Their faces will try to hide behind their hands and behind the rocks and behind the trees. They will try to hide, but there will be no place to go. For the light, akin to no other, just IS. The light will follow into the deepest and darkest parts of all the earth. And it will be the age of wonder. For man will wonder about these times that are come upon the earth.

Here history will repeat itself, for Light came into the world, and man chose and preferred the darkness. And so again, some will simply put on colored glasses against the light. They will quickly reach for thick glasses of despair and loneliness, glasses of rebellion and unbelief. And as incredible as it might seem, these glasses will filter out the greatest light that the world has ever known or seen.

Preface

Those who choose not to be blinded by the light, but who look beyond the light into what it is revealing, these will see the dying and perishing pick up the glasses. They will see their arms go out and their hands grasp for the tools of darkness. And there will be no way, no reason, no ability to separate them from their implements of darkness, for the choice will be made. And quickly, almost as quickly as the light comes, they will grab and push, and they will secure their blankets and their glasses of darkness to protect themselves against the light.

But there will be many men who will throw their glasses away, for they will be mesmerized by the light. They will be attracted to the light. They will be drawn by the light. And they will look and they will peer into the blinding, stunning light, and their eyes and their senses will be seared, and they will no longer see any of the things that they have always seen before, for they will be seared forever.

And after the first moments of shock have passed, they will see past that wave of light, through that wave of light, into another world. A world of miracles. A world where the Word transcends the flesh. A world where the Word creates, even as it created when the earth was a vast and dark void, formless and quiet. The Word will create before the very eyes of man. The eyes that have been seared by this new light will see a forming out of those things which are unseen. They will see coming into existence those things which are seen. Where for many years there was an empty eye socket, as the Word of faith is spoken in this season of accelerated growth, there will form a new eye: a new retina, a new pupil, a new eyelid, new eyelashes.

New limbs will grow, and those who have put on their glasses and smothered themselves under their blankets will NOT SEE. They simply WILL NOT SEE. Deception always finds its own answers. Deception always seeks and finds the path along which to run away, to its own way. For even as those who seek after Me as after silver and hidden treasure and find Me," saith the Lord, "those in the darkness who desire and seek deception will find. Those who desire and seek unbelief will find. Those who desire and seek rebellion will find.

For there is coming the matrix [Christ] and a pinnacle [highest place], a place that mankind has always desired to go, and tried to climb to, and could never reach. The pinnacle, out of the midst of the being of Mount Zion, will be reached in a day, in an hour, in a moment, literally in the twinkling of an eye. And there will be change, great and vast and mighty change. You all shall be changed, in the twinkling of an eye. For the trumpet is sounding, the trumpet of the voice of the prophets, and change, CHANGE, **CHANGE** is in the air. Smell it, hear it, speak it, look upon it, for it is here. Gaze into that which your eyes cannot perceive. Hear and look into that which seems to be a wall, which seems to be a cloud, a haze, for it is a wall and a haze and a wave of light," saith the Lord.

"And the plowman, with his hand upon the plow, will look ahead down the furrows, and he'll see the haze coming. And to him, it might look like a wave of dust. But his step will not falter and his eyes will not turn aside; his tread will be firm and his pace steady, as he walks down the furrows of the freshly turned earth. He has a job to do, and the time is short. His step will not falter, and as the cloud nears, closer, closer, he will brace into the wind, and he will hear its whistle. But his heart will be fixed, and he will not fear, nor will he turn aside. For he is going on an inner clock, an inner watch, on inner orders, and he will tread straight ahead. He will tread straight into the cloud, the veritable cloud of light.

And as the cloud—which didn't appear to be light at all—envelops him, and the plow, and the field, and the furrows, and all that the eye can see, he will not falter. His hand will stay upon the handle and his tread will go straight ahead. And once the cloud envelops him, and only then, he will perceive that it is a cloud of glory. And his heart will be fixed, and his face and his feet will go straight ahead.

For now, in the cloud of glory, plowing will continue. But it will be totally and literally without effort. For the cloud is a consuming cloud, consuming all the flesh. Consuming all the negative in man's emotions and will. The cloud takes man into a realm where he will continue in the task that he has been given, but the Word is made flesh before his very eyes.

Preface

And the plowman will notice the reaper at his side, and the sower of the seed, but it will no longer be clear who comes first or who comes last, who is here now and who was here past. It will no longer be clear whose task is here and whose task is there. And man will no longer fear that he will clatter and come and shatter the dreams of God. For the plowman and the sower and the reaper now work and labor together in the vineyards of their God and in His strength and in His power and in the cloud of the effervescent light, the shimmering rainbow lightning clarity of the cloud of great glory. Joy will be the very air that they breathe. Delight will be a skip in the step and a lilt in the heart as the plow cuts effortlessly through hard and crusted earth.

And the astonished eye of the plowman will see seed sown and scattered before the plow gets to the sower, but it won't matter. There is no longer time. There is no longer the "right order" for doing things. The seed of the Word will not return void, nor will it be snatched away. The army of the Lord, an army of sowers, reapers, and harvesters, an army of plowmen and waterers, and carriers of the light and the fire: THAT ARMY WILL DEVOUR THE EARTH. It will run upon the walls and the hills and the valleys of the earth, faster than light, deeper than darkness, more profound than sound. The army will advance and advance and advance, devouring the earth.

And these individuals that run upon the walls will no longer be carrying candles into the darkness. They will no longer be carrying torches lit with matches, lit with flint and tinder wet and reluctant to bear the light. They will no longer carry the light in their hand or wonder where the light comes from or how they can make it happen. Instead, the light will carry them; they'll ride upon it, and stride upon it, they will swim in it and walk upon it. The light will be the very air that they breathe and the wind at their back blowing them on toward their goal. For with the advancing great army of the Lord is the cloud of great glory, the cloud of awesome light, and they advance together.

All of the weapons of the enemy that have seemed so powerful:

    alcohol

        drugs

            physical abuses

                the murderous intents that have filled the hearts of men," saith the Lord, "those weapons will be pitiful and small and ineffectual, child's play, before the great and awesome army of the Lord, before the cloudburst of laser light, the light of My glory," saith the Lord.

"And their weapons will fall, forgotten, by the side of the road, as drug addicts and prostitutes and murderers are enveloped and consumed by My light. They will leap from their beds and from their hells of darkness and join the army. They will join the relentless pace, the steady advance, the persistent onslaught of an army consumed by light, an army that no longer fears the darkness, sees the darkness, or smells the darkness; an army not even aware of the darkness and the sin. There will be no consciousness of sin, for the army is consumed by light, by purity and by power.

And they relentlessly march onward in a straight and a unified path, not veering to the left or to the right.

And there is one standing order:

ADVANCE!"

INTRODUCTION

On a particular day, many, many years ago, a man called Jesus got into a boat and pushed away from the shore. The crowds had so pressed to hear the words of life, that he taught them from the water. He spoke in simple words, painting pictures with stories of everyday life. The parables were so profound in meaning that they still speak today with the same fresh and powerful blade of Truth. They show us pictures of God's ways and purposes in the hearts of men.

Many times, Jesus spoke of the seed and the ground, the vineyard and the vinedresser, the wheat, the wine, and oil. The parable of the sower speaks of plowing, sowing, and reaping. Jesus demonstrated practically with loaves and fishes to a people rigid and hard of heart that He IS the Bread of Life. They didn't always understand what He said, but the power of God the Father drew them in spite of themselves. There was hunger inside them that they didn't understand. They were struggling to survive in a world they didn't understand, and they were drawn by the authority and life and hope in this stranger from Galilee.

Sadly today, people are still running to drugs and alcohol, to psychics, prophets, and anyone who seems to be able to give them hope and direction in a confused, complex and dark world. They are hungry and confused in a confusing age. They desperately need the profound spiritual revelation so radical to the religious world and the unbelievers which Jesus revealed in that long ago most significant hour, veiled in parables and dark sayings.

Because it has been given to you to know the mysteries of the kingdom of heaven, but to them it has not been given. For whoever has, to him more will be given, and he will have abundance; but whoever does not have, even what he has will be taken away from him. Therefore I speak to them in parables, because seeing they do not see, and hearing they do not hear, nor do they understand. Matt. 13:11-13

HE WHO HAS EARS TO HEAR, LET HIM HEAR!

I grew up hearing that scripture and it got very familiar. I felt I had ears, and, feeling righteous as a regular church-goer, that I WAS hearing—more than most. But I was only hearing words, not revelation knowledge. I was not hearing the Spirit of wisdom and revelation and power. In these last days we must HEAR what the Spirit is saying as the parables and dark sayings of Jesus are opened to those hungry to hear and see with the perspective of the Most High God.

God is speaking with the trumpet sounds of His prophets in these last days, and the moving of the masses to hear the voices of His prophets indicates that they are beginning to hear heavenly sounds, and are responding in the only way many are able to at this time. This is a time to clearly understand harvest. It is upon us. What does it mean? To comprehend harvest, and this most unique time, we must first have clear comprehension of the steps leading to harvest—plowing, planting, watering, and increase. "The plowman shall overtake the reaper…" How can this be possible? It indicates that all the steps will happen at once. It suggests acceleration. Thank God. We all like things to be fast. But are we ready and can we handle it?

Darkness is getting darker and light more brilliant. Shaking is the result. Signs and wonders of the culmination of the ages are beginning to manifest. Dangers and traps are laid by darkness for teachers of light. Adulation and grasping of the masses toward workers of miracles, and jealousy and judgment toward the same cause great upheavals leading to apostasy, deception, and disappointment. Ministry is changing: will ministers change with it? The ages are changing: will the masses turn toward the light? New levels of light are awaking the church. Will the Body of Christ change with them?

This is a critical and strategic hour of awakening, repositioning, and preparation. This season of intense growth and expansion is compelling us into maturity. There must come a heart for the deposit of God in others (the seed of Life), rather than so much consciousness of self, self-absorption,

and self-adulation. We must mature into the heart of the Father of Nations—
the Lord of the harvest Himself.

As the season of the plowman overtaking the reaper comes, enlightened
perspective will come to every part of God's army to recognize and value
His purpose in others. Unity of the Body will manifest as vision broadens
and competition ceases. Each will value the other and their function, no
longer even noticing elevation, favor, or persecution. In this critical time,
the Body of Christ must lay down their arms against one another and unite
in vision, revelation, and purpose, counting it all joy that the testing of faith
leads to the perfection and fullness in us of Him who IS our joy and crown.

Our task is before us: to join the Lord of the Harvest in plowing,
planting, and reaping the greatest harvest the world has ever seen. The
Kingdom of God is manifesting in all of its fullness! Great light is upon the
horizon of our lives. Our eyes must adjust to new levels of light. Our hearts
must thrill to the tasks before us, even as we accelerate and go forward into
this great season of Harvest!

I

THE SOIL AND THE CRUST

Then He said to His disciples, "The harvest is [indeed] plentiful, but the workers are few. So pray to the Lord of the harvest to send out workers into His harvest." Matt. 9:37-38 AMP

Central thought: God's creation, His Beloved, will manifest unprecedented life, propagating and releasing fruitfulness and abundance. The garden of the Lord will bring to Him great delight. All the plowing and tilling of the soil, all the sowing and care, will take us through into the Most Holy Place resulting in the joy of communion and fulfillment.

NATURE OF THE FIELD

Are you a sower in God's fields? As His child, yes! Are you a field of His at the same time? Yes! You and I as children of the living God are both at once, in this time of increasing harvest. We go out to plow, even as we ourselves are being plowed. And as we go out into the fields of the world we find different kinds, different types of fields so to speak, and in times of great harvest often they are fields not like those we have ever seen. Old ways of sowing or plowing may not be up to date or effective in every place or every person. We have to sow by the spirit, plow by the spirit, led as always by the wisdom of Holy Spirit. This is a time to function in the spirit with increased sensitivity and determination.

So often we have tried to scatter seed without the least understanding of the particular field where we are, the state of the soil, or who has gone before us or what they may have done. Even more often we try to fix all those around us without examining the state of our own heart's field and changes that should be made there first. The parables of Jesus concerning these issues are both simple and complex. God is sharpening our perspective!

Behold the sower went out to sow. Matt. 13:3

How did the sower in this parable feel about the place he was about to sow his precious seed? Good farmers thrill to see rich, fertile, tilled earth, ready for planting. Much like mothers who see their children obedient and sweet-spirited and teachable, farmers derive immense satisfaction in the progress and development of fruitful land. Value is placed on the quality and content of the earth, as well as the present condition of the soil. Planting and harvesting only thrive in abundance when the conditions of the soil are right.

And others fell on the GOOD SOIL, and yielded a crop, some a hundredfold, some sixty, and some thirty. Matt. 13:8

I often wonder how the Lord finds me, the soil in which He has placed His treasure. Does He find me soft and malleable and ready for his seed, or hard and rocky and a lot of work? Does He have a lot of work ahead to make me different? What IS good soil in our world? Is it dark, rich black, bright red, sandy, grainy? Is one texture better than another? Should it be soft or hard? Can you identify "good soil" by the outward appearance? Does good soil need less fertilizer? Does it require less maintenance?

Farmers will tell us that good soil is soil which protects and nourishes the seed and anchors the growing roots. It is soil that gracefully and constantly changes with the need of the seasons and the will of the plowman. The entire purpose in all the care and tilling of the soil is to preserve and encourage the seed, giving it stability. The dirt must be soft and pliable, housing the minerals and water which encourage the seed to grow.

Many days I don't feel pliable. I don't feel soft and trainable. And I definitely don't feel inclined toward being plowed up, dug into, and mashed flat. So many of the necessary activities involved in making me ready to grow God's fruit don't sound enjoyable, and experience usually confirms that idea. We all know that whom the Lord loves He chastens disciplines and trains. It just doesn't make it any easier to know that sometimes. But I definitely DO want to fulfill my destiny. I want to change and grow into His image. So I sometimes reluctantly pray, go ahead and plow me up, Lord, and make me fertile soil for your planting.

What is the condition of our own soil, but at the same time, what is the state of the ground we have come to till?

THREE PARTS

In natural soil you have three parts: clay to bind the soil together, sand which aerates the soil, and humus for the organic matter and minerals. Good soil must have a proper combination of each. All clay produces rock, all sand and the earth won't hold the water; all humus ends in rot. The three parts must be carefully blended and plowed together, united in the common purpose: housing the seed.

There is definitely a parallel between the three parts of natural soil, and the three-fold nature of man.

> Now may the God of peace Himself sanctify you entirely; and may your spirit and soul and body be preserved complete, without blame at the coming of our Lord Jesus Christ. 1 Thess. 5:23

Just like natural soil, we are three parts, body, soul and spirit. After we are born again, all three parts are in a state of the constant change necessary to nurture and mature the Seed of Life inside us. Clay can be likened to the body. Many of us have experienced total obsession with the physical body. All purpose and activity is directed toward this one part of an indivisible three-part being, often to the point that one or both of the other parts virtually disappear. The hardness that results in the soul and spirit from that kind of imbalance is much like that all-clay rock.

So many of us are preoccupied with development and adornment of the body. Beauty is sought after with every means available. My best friend growing up had red hair, green eyes and dimples. I had hair and eyes the color of mud. When the boys seemed to prefer her over me, I naturally assumed that mud color was not the ideal, preferred by all those with discernment. I prayed every night for red hair, green eyes and dimples, but brown is what I have retained, all these years. But when all of our time, energy and resources are focused on the physical body, the two other very important parts begin to show neglect.

Sand is like the soul part of man—his mind, will and emotions. God blew into the body of man the breath of life, and man's soul was born. But after the fall, the mind, will, and emotions of man fell along with his body. Scripture says that the carnal, or un-regenerated, mind of man is at enmity with God. Paul tells us therefore to put on the mind of Christ.

"All sand" can be likened to the soul-conscious, mind-oriented person, who has difficulty holding the living water of the Spirit. Great intellects have much difficulty accepting the things of the spirit. When the mind part of man is deified, humanism rears up like a mighty dragon, and man's pride and will are like a run-away stallion, pursuing a wild and unrestrained course toward destruction. Sand alone, or the carnal soul of man, cannot comprehend the things of the Spirit.

Humus is the enriching portion of natural earth. It is the part that causes life to flourish, and can be likened to the spirit part of man. Humus must have sand and clay to enrich, or it rots. So the spirit portion of man in this earth must have body and soul to complete itself. In this earth in partnership with God, we cannot find expression without an earthen vessel, or a body.

And so we see that soil, that is GOOD soil, must have clay for substance (a body), sand to aerate it (a soul connecting the spirit and body), and humus to give it life (the richness of the Word, the minerals of life— the Spirit). We are the Body and He is the Head. He has put His treasure, His inheritance, into earthen vessels, that the excellence of the power may be of God, and not of man (2 Cor. 4:7).

So to recap: just like natural earth being tilled and cultivated and changed, man has three parts in a continual state of renovation. We are in a state of being changed from glory to glory into His image, as a new creature in Christ (2 Cor. 5:17). When we are saved, we have a newly reborn spirit, joined to His. We have a soul which is being daily transformed, mind, will and emotions. Our mind learns to operate with the mind of Christ and our will is transformed into His will. Then there are our often out-of-control emotions (selfishness, hatred, pettiness, greed, etc.) which must change into His: love, joy, peace, longsuffering, meekness, temperance, faith. Our body is also being changed. We are learning to put it in subjection to the spirit. Our spirit must rule soul and body with Christ as our Lord.

As harvesters, we are working with many others in the fields of the world in all levels of this process, requiring us to draw on the Lord's wisdom in all endeavors even as we ourselves are growing into maturity.

DEATH VS LIFE

Even as natural earth becomes hard, rebellious and resistant to the efforts of the farmer, so our personal soil, our inner man, resists being tilled and cultivated, as the great sword or blade of the Word plows us up. As we allow our three parts to be changed into His image, we become aware of the definite opposition to this process. The war of the law of sin and death is in operation in our various parts. Our un-regenerated earth wars against the law of God in our inner man, the seed of life (Romans 7:23-25). So as we prepare our soil for the growth of the spirit we, by the Spirit, put to death the deeds of the body, and live.

This is not a pretty process! Death is never fun. It is often painful, humiliating, and undignified. We don't like to die! But, more on that later. While the soul and body struggle with the death process, the spirit (the humus—the minerals, the life) gets excited about new life. This causes war. Learning in a very practical way to allow the richness of the spirit (humus) to invade and give life to the carnal mind, will, and emotions is sometimes a challenge. "I would that you walk not after the flesh, but after the spirit" (Rom. 8:4). This is not a simple process to learn.

Learning to speak by His Spirit with my mouth, for example—saying what the Father says, like Jesus, can be a frightening phenomenon to my natural understanding. Fear rears its uncomfortable head all too often. But God has not given us a spirit of fear, but of love, power and a sound mind (2 Tim. 1:7). Fear is death in operation within a vessel designed for life. It is overwhelming to know that the Lord of Hosts can use my mouth to speak, for example as He used Isaiah, Jeremiah, Deborah, David, Paul, Luke, John, and countless others across the ages. You are probably as I am—constantly fighting the fear that you are going to speak in the name of the Lord and make a terrible mistake. I have never doubted God. My doubt has always been of myself. I am afraid of harming someone or giving wrong direction. But we must not allow a spirit of fear to interfere with God's purpose in and through us.

I used to be terrified of flying. I just hated it. The slightest bit of turbulence and I'd sit there terrified—what my husband calls a "white-knuckled flyer." We went to Pittsburgh once and when we got about two hundred miles away, there were horrible storms surrounding the city on three sides. They decided to go west and all the way around Pittsburgh before they could come in from the east. It was the roughest plane flight that I have ever experienced. I tried reciting Psalm 46: "Though the earth should change and slip into the heart of the sea, I will not fear . . ." I quoted and quoted and when the fear didn't go away I finally decided to pretend I was on a train. I closed my eyes, trying to hear that click, click, click of the wheels. The mighty woman of faith and power was on her way to minister!

Many times people noticing my heavy travel schedule would ask, "How do you feel about flying so much?" I always replied, "I hate flying; I loathe it! I would rather do anything than fly!" Finally, after getting my attention, the Lord said, "It's not flying you hate. It's fear." I thought about it and I realized the profound truth. It is the fear that we hate, not necessarily the thing itself. And so every time I got on a plane from then on, I began to bind the spirit of fear and all the manifestations of it. Each time the turbulence came, I "bound" the spirit of fear.

Gradually, several trips later, I realized that I was no longer afraid. You know how it is when you receive healing over a period of time until you forget about it and then you realize one day that you are healed. Well, that's the way it was. One day I realized that I was beginning to enjoy flying. I actually enjoyed watching the ground fall away. Even landing—I was beginning to enjoy it! I was a miracle. The new earth had just had a "death" stone removed from its depths, and I was rejoicing in new life in the care of the husbandman.

As we are consistently putting away the deeds of death and darkness, we are growing into the life of God, growing into His image, indeed sons of God, and children of the Spirit of Life. We learn to speak His words, think His thoughts, and do what He does--just as Jesus did! Literally, we learn to walk in another realm--the realm of the Spirit.

FLESH VS SPIRIT

Jesus, the good farmer of the soil of our life, is teaching us to allow the spirit (the humus!) to aerate and transform our flesh. Remember, there is great opposition to this process! I don't want to do what I know to do, and I do that which I know I should not. Basically, the apostle Paul said that first in Romans 7.

As we walk in the Spirit, most of our battle comes in the unseen realm. We may think that circumstances are making us miserable; we may think people around us are the problem. But literally we are fighting three things at once: the flesh, the devil and the world. The reason Jesus spoke in dark sayings and types and shadows, was so that we could look past natural circumstances and see the Spirit of God through them.

Being convinced that the most solid thing about our lives is the ground under our feet may change drastically when we go to an earthquake prone region. The ground isn't solid at all when it begins to shake. It graphically illustrates the contrast between what we look at as the "real," stable world, and that kingdom which cannot be shaken. That's why the Lord would take a parable or a dark saying and use the natural things of the world to get the attention of the people so that they could see. The disciples were physical people, mostly fishermen and carpenters, rough and ready, brawny men that were used to working in a natural world. They were bound by their sight and their feeling and their senses—by their flesh.

We don't realize how cushioned we tend to be at home. Every sense is petted and cosseted. We can be so satiated with our physical senses that our spiritual man is neglected and ignored, seemingly weak and underdeveloped. It is all too easy to lie around and watch television and become a vegetable. But we must learn to walk in the Spirit. We must decrease so that He may increase, that we may become strengthened with mighty power in our inner, new man.

We learn to look beyond what is perceived and experienced by the natural and soulish senses, and discern the still small voice of the Spirit. Looking past the whirlwind and the fire to peer into the realm of the Spirit is much like getting our attention off of the soil and the look of the field and onto the whole point of everything: The Seed.

OLD MAN/NEW MAN: NEW EARTH

When our spirit is born again we become a new creature with the divine Seed, the Spirit of God living inside of us. Old things are passed away and all things are become new. But we must learn that it is new. Old dirt has to go, and new soil is being changed out! We must learn to put on the new and put off the old. And, like the Apostle Paul, we cry out at the seeming war within ourselves.

> For the mind set on the flesh is death, but the mind set on the Spirit is life and peace, because the mind set on the flesh is hostile toward God; for it does not subject itself to the law of God, for it is not even able to do so; and those who are in the flesh cannot please God. Rom. 8:6-8.

The Lord desires to translate us from operating in principles of law into the grace that Christ died to give. We cannot make ourselves die. We cannot make ourselves live. But what we can do is submit to the dealings of God and His choices for our lives instead of our own. Law causes us to make choices according to duty or the opinions of others. Then we can be satisfied with our obedience and the end result is just self-righteousness rather than transformation into His image.

But when the Lord takes out the plow, He begins to break up all that self-righteousness to the point that we realize there isn't anything WE can do at all. The only way to Life that we can choose is to ALLOW His plowing and His moving in our lives, because the work, the battle is His. We still have to go to war, but the battle is the Lord's and the outcome is already finished. It is not our work, our labor, but His. "Except the Lord builds the house, they labor in vain who build it" (Psalm 127:1).

SEASONS OF PROGRESSION

We are all on a journey in our spiritual walk with the Lord, just like a natural seed buried in the earth. That burial is only the beginning of a marvelous process, which from beginning to end can be characterized by one word: change. The seed continually grows and changes through stage after stage until it bursts through the earth to continue changing. So there are experiences or progressions of change in the spiritual development of our relationship with Him. Recognizing these seasons often helps us understand not only where we've come from, but the place where we are and where we are headed.

I once had a progressive vision in a meeting during highly anointed worship. The result of this vision was to give me hope for the future—hope that where I am will change, that there is always more in God, and that if I will just submit to the plow of God in my life, I will know more and more of Him, and I will dwell in increasingly close communion with Him.

My spiritual vision was in three parts or scenes, which the Lord changed much as one would change slides in a PowerPoint.

In the first scene, I was climbing up a steep, almost vertical, and rocky mountain. It was dark and windy with rain blowing in great gusts, and the rocks were slippery. There were no easy footholds, and my grasp was uncertain. I was very tired and discouraged but determined. I would slip and bruise and then have to recover the ground. There was no top in sight. In despair I knew this was my walk with the Lord, and I asked Him, "Is this all there is?"

When the question was asked, that slide disappeared and the next slide came in. On the next slide I was waltzing with the Lord in the midst of clouds which billowed in and around us as we danced. I had on a long chiffon dress which floated and swirled with our movement. The scene was one of joy and carefreeness. The interesting thing was that this scene kept superimposing on the first as though I could not let go of the first, or didn't realize that I didn't have to go back. As I concentrated on the clouds, the first scene gradually left altogether. I watched the dance for a long time and finally became aware of a faint but hazy question deep within myself. I asked the Lord again, "Is this all there is?" And so when my question came again, He took that slide out and the next slide came in.

The Lord was carrying me in an undefined space of great light, almost as though we were walking through many concentrated spotlights. Shot through the light sources were rainbow-like prisms. He and I were transparent, like the appearance of bubbles when light shines on them and iridescence radiates. I saw us from the back as though He had gone past, carrying me. My dress fell in graceful folds from His arms and my hair hung long and loose, almost golden in the light. There was LOVE in nearly tangible form. As He walked carrying me in the glory, my image was merged into His. Our individual outlines were still distinct, but merged into each other: separate, yet one. There was no succeeding scene, and I watched until I could no longer see the vision.

SCENE ONE

As I sought the Lord about it, He reminded me that we could be said to have a first day experience when we are saved. Using the three places in the Tabernacle of Moses in our analogy, we know that one comes first into the Outer Court where the Lamb is sacrificed, signifying Jesus, and the Lamb that was slain from the foundation of the world. We are crucified with the Lamb which is Christ and we put away that old man, the old nature, and become a new creature—our salvation or "born again" experience. I don't remember not being saved, since I grew up on the front pew of the church. It seems that I always knew my Savior. But with many there is a distinct and sharp change, from one life to another.

In the Outer Court there is natural light. We are living on the earth and our main tendency is to look at everything around us with "natural light." We are still trying to achieve with our soul power, effort and striving. Often because of lack of revelation of Who He is and therefore who we are IN Him, we fall back into old habits and ways of doing things: "you get where you are by what you put into it," and competition, "no pain, no gain." I know that I am supposed to read the Bible so I will try two hours a day. I did an hour yesterday; I will try two hours today.

Because of trying to accomplish spiritual goals in the power of the flesh, we get hurt, discouraged, and disillusioned. Holding onto worldly attitudes and desires, we open the door to evil influences, bringing more struggles and pain on ourselves. So we are clawing our way by sheer determination up the mountain while continually fighting wind, rain and storms. This is a great picture of the seed fighting its own environment instead of resting in the knowledge that the farmer will take care of all.

SCENE TWO

We can move into a second experience in God and be baptized in the Holy Spirit. This can be likened to the Inner Court of the Tabernacle, also called the Holy Place. When you move into a second day or second room experience, the room with the golden lampstand, you have new revelation, new eyes, illumination of things hitherto unexplained. Also in the Holy Place we discover the table of showbread and we begin to eat the bread of life and we begin to change. When you eat, food becomes a part of you and you reflect that which you eat.

It is here in this next experience after being saved, the Baptism in the Holy Spirit, that we have the opportunity to begin to speak in another language. When I received it, I thought the end had come. I could not imagine there being anything after it. The excitement of moving into another realm with the Lord of Glory cannot be compared to anything on earth. As a result, many who receive the Baptism in the Holy Spirit go crazy and offend nearly everyone around. I did that along with the best of them. I probably didn't do that quite as much as my sister did because I was a lot more inhibited than she was. We didn't think she was crazy, we KNEW she was crazy! But she was ahead of me in knowledge and experience of the Lord, and had I had more revelation at the time, I wouldn't have been so quick with my opinions.

After receiving the Baptism in the Holy Spirit, reading the Bible is suddenly the most exciting thing—words just jump off the page! You pray for parking places and immediately they're there. Sudden understanding of the ways and acts of God provides constant excitement. Then we begin to worship.

Just at the next door, still in the Holy Place, we find the altar of incense. It is here that we began to worship in spirit and in truth. I learned to raise my hands. It was so exciting when I got my hands past my shoulders. It took time to break me out of so much shyness and self-consciousness. But I learned that one cannot be self-conscious and GOD-conscious at the same time. Abandon in expressing my adoration in scriptural ways of worship joined my love of prayer and I began to dance with the Lord in another realm full of joy and peace.

After the Lord showed me the three scenes, I had a dream. In it, I saw the Inner Court or Holy Place. There was the biggest party going on in there. People were dancing and having fun; they were laughing and filled with great joy. As the wonderful party continued, I noticed, hidden behind all the activity, the door into the Most Holy Place (the third and last room). It was closed and obviously they had forgotten it was there. The people were just having fun partying in the Holy Place and that was all there was.

When I woke up, I said, "God, they have become content. They have made a tabernacle and camped in the Inner Court, dancing with the Lord." Having fun. Partying. And they have forgotten that there is more. Either that or they don't want take the effort that will be necessary because they know what they went through to get as far as the inner court. They have chosen forgetfulness, but God's Word says, "He will revive us after two days; He will raise us up on the third day that we may live before Him. So let us know, let us press on to know the Lord. His going forth is as certain as the dawn; and He will come to us like the rain, like the spring rain watering the earth" (Hosea 6:2-3). Let us press onward. In my vision, even after the joy of Scene Two, I still asked, "Is this all there is?" There is a third Court in the house: the Most Holy Place.

SCENE THREE

Throughout the Scriptures we find over and over that the third day was significant. Jesus was raised on the third day; Lazarus was raised on the third day. Hezekiah was healed on the third day. A day is as a thousand years with the Lord and it has been two thousand years since Jesus came the first time. So we in the corporate Body of Christ could be said to be moving into a third day experience.

In the Most Holy Place there lies only one object: the Ark of the Covenant. To the Israelites, this ark was literally the Shekinah Presence of the Most High. It is made of wood and covered on the outside and on the inside with gold. Wood symbolizes humanity. The prophetic imagery of this is so amazing. As we grow in the spirit, our humanity is covered inside and out with the gold of His purity and deity.

Christ said, "I am in you and you are in Me." When I questioned the Lord about it, He showed me a visual picture of what He meant. I saw the Lord standing, holding a suit of clothes. It was all in one piece, like the pajama suit that babies wear, with feet, hands and hood attached, and a zipper up the middle. The suit, which was transparent and hung limply in His Hands like a snake skin, looked like Lora. He unzipped it and He put His arm in my arm, His other arm in mine, He put His legs in my legs, and He zipped it up and He looked like me. And He said, "This is my earth suit." So He is in us and we are in Him. Gold, wood and gold.

When we come into the Most Holy Place, we are alone with God. No carnal thinking, no I've got to's, no duty, no guts, no determination, no striving, and no strain. Nothing exists there but God. So those who have been in the Holy Place and are still striving with the arm of flesh find themselves in the unique position of flitting back and forth from room to room as the situation presents itself. We know that in Christ we are all three of these. But as we continue to put off the old, there often is still a looking back, when in the completeness of union there is only ONE. We and God

13

have become One. We are no longer double minded. No wavering—in one place one moment and in another the next.

We cannot come into the Most Holy Place dragging anything that cannot be one with the Lord of Glory. He cannot become one with our striving. He cannot become one with our hurt. He cannot become one with our insecurity. He cannot become one with our pride. He cannot become one with our fear. So we must allow the plow of God to plow us up and turn the soil and mix us with Himself so that the seed that is sown can do whatever it needs to do to propagate the earth. We are being tilled and cultivated into a new place with the Lord.

In the third scene of my vision, in the new realm of radiant and effervescent light (not natural light, but the Light of the Lamb), He carries us in indescribable union. There is no longer even the awareness of other realms. There is no desire, longing, or time, because He fulfills completely, forever. We have entered into His rest, into communion with our Beloved where we take pleasure in His Presence and He in ours.

In the Song of Solomon, the Lord refers to wine in speaking of the intimacy of expressed love. With that in mind, I find it very interesting in the context of our keynote scripture:

> Behold, the days are coming, says the Lord, when the plowman shall overtake the reaper, and the treader of grapes him who sows seed; the mountains shall drip with sweet wine, and all the hills shall flow with it. Amos 9:13 NKJV

Several years ago, I discovered a piece of material in a fabric store in Washington, D.C. As I looked at the gorgeous fabric, I thought I heard the voice of the Lord say, "Your lips drip sweet wine." At this time, I had been making banners and dance garments depicting various scriptures, so I was not surprised at the unusual thought. The material was very interesting; it was deep fuchsia colored chiffon with golden splashes through it. Purple trails ran down the cloth intermittently, combining with the gold to literally look like the dripping of wine and honey. There was an accompanying fabric of heavily beaded and sequined fuchsia lace that looked like grapes and flowers. I bought both pieces of expensive material and then didn't know what to do with them. So I put them in the closet for three years.

Finally, I felt the direction of the Lord that it was time to deal with that fabric. As I studied Song of Solomon, I found the scriptures, "Thy lips, O my spouse, drop as the honeycomb: honey and milk are under thy tongue; and the smell of thy garments is like the smell of Lebanon" (Song 4:11, KJV), and "The fragrance of your breath like apples, and the roof of your mouth like the best wine" (Song 7:8b-9a, NKJ). Although the literal phrase, "Your lips drip sweet wine," is never actually used in the Bible, I knew that I was on a path led by the Lord. So I began to study the words, "drip sweet wine," and came to "the mountains shall drip sweet wine." In the Word, wine is symbolic of the joy of the Lord and the blood of the Lamb.

So in our present study, the mountains (the *new earth*—we, His treasure in earthen vessels, His new creation) will drip with sweet wine and all the hills shall flow with it. God's creation, His Beloved if you will, will manifest unprecedented life, propagating and releasing fruitfulness and abundance. The garden of the Lord will bring to Him great delight. All the plowing and tilling of the soil, all the sowing and care, will take us through the Holy Place experience into the Most Holy Place resulting in the joy of communion and fulfillment.

THE CRUST OF THE EARTH

So we, as good soil should, are earnestly apprehending by faith that new realm where the spirit transcends the flesh, life triumphs over death, and the new man puts to death the deeds of the old and lives. This process involves continual tilling of the soil to receive, nurture, and CONTINUE to nurture, the seed.

Behold, the sower went out to sow. And as he sowed, some seeds fell beside the road, and the birds came and ate them up.
Matt.13:3-4

What happens on a wayside, on the side of the road? The soil on the side of the road is hard, packed, and strewn with rocks thrown from the passage of many feet. It is a place of ceaseless activity. The birds will come because they know that nothing can live there. They know that the seed can't take root and thus they can pick up all the seed they want. If we allow the ceaseless passage of anything and everything through our minds and lives, then we are become like a public roadside, blown about by every wind of doctrine and hardened in the process. We go here and there in ceaseless activity, labor, works, sweat and toil. We have provided a perfect opportunity for the fowl of the air, for the darts of the enemy to come in and steal the seed. When we set our mind on the Lord, and focus our lives on His word, His word lives and takes root in our hearts and becomes part of us. It is our choice whether His seed is stolen in our lives.

> And others fell upon the rocky places, where they did not have much soil; and immediately they sprang up, because they had no depth of soil. But when the sun had risen, they were scorched; and because they had no root, they withered away. Matt. 13:5-6

For all kinds of reasons, hardness forms in the soil of our lives— unbelief, doubt, bitterness, and hurt. All of these things form a hard place, a kind of CRUST over our heart. When that hard stony place forms and the seed comes, there may be enough dirt scattered there that the seed can spring up for a time, but then when the sun comes out, there is no healthy root. Roots must go down in the earth to get water, nutrients, and all of the things that make life possible. But if there is no deep root, the sun withers it. Without being rooted and grounded in the love of God with its healing rivers, the seed of God will be scorched in the light of the fire of the Son of God, and just like the natural seed in the parable, will wither.

Hardness or crust is death residing in the soil. "Today, if you hear His voice, do not harden your hearts" (Heb. 4:7). This hardness, this death, is a manifestation of the curse. It is living in the old nature, the old unregenerated, un-reborn dead state, without the consistent care of the husbandman. Part of the curse on the earth after the fall of Adam was that the earth became hard and rebellious, resisting the propagation of all life and seed. This hardness, rebellion, or CRUST, is broken up by the plow.

The protection found in the unity of the Body of Christ and the continual plowing and tilling of the soil of our lives through praise and worship will prevent the forming of crust and hardness of heart. The shepherd, or pastor, is one of the wielders of the plow of the Word. In a local church we join together to give and receive living water. God speaks to the flock through the voice of the shepherds, imparting fresh oil and anointing wounds. This is a day when the great Plowman of God is taking out His sharp instrument and destroying the manifestations of a curse that was destroyed for all time on Calvary.

Because crust contains salt and minerals, a thick crust will cause the earth to become too salty for the seed. Have you ever been around someone who is so salty that you can hardly stand their presence? Some destroy their marriages because they become so salty and self-righteous that they can't be lived with. If you have too much salt you can't eat your food. Salt must be used lightly, with temperance. The plow takes that crust and cuts into it, turning it over and mixing it, so that it can receive the seed. In mixing that hardness and death (the death of our humanity), with the water and breath of life, the crust actually fertilizes the rest of the soil, producing much richer soil than had there been no death involved. Selah!

So the soil must rejoice and say, "I know that if I have a root of rejection, the Husbandman is coming. I rejoice that He will give me more attention today than yesterday because He has work to do in me." That is the attitude of good soil. The attitude of poor, untilled soil is, I am always sad. My life is sad because people are mean to me. My family hates me. My friends hate me. Everyone hates me. All these things that have happened to me are not fair. God is not fair. He wouldn't have let this happen to me if He really loved me.

Before we know it, we have spoken into being every other root of rejection and spirit of bitterness and resentment in the whole farm and they have all concentrated their attention right on our little plot of ground. We have given life and power to what should be dead issues by embracing negative thought patterns. Practically speaking, we must allow the plowing of the Lord to come into our lives so that we can be good soil, the planting of the Lord.

There are times when I feel that problems I am working on are actually multiplying. They seem to grow in intensity and dimension instead of being dealt with finally and put away. The reason for that feeling is because God is accelerating His work. As the plow goes into the ground and turns up the soil, problems surface. The great Plowman is taking the sharp blade of the Spirit and cutting deep into our lives, plowing and turning over the earth, preparing and renewing our earth, and transforming it into the kind of soil that so delights the husbandman.

We are being plowed, planted, and harvested into a new dimension. We are going to walk as a unified Army in a place of unprecedented light, a place of great exposure. If you have felt exposed, if you have felt that things were surfacing in your life that you thought were long dead, if you have felt the Body of Christ being exposed, if you have seen ministry and church leaders falling into sin and exposed publicly in national headlines—then it is because light is bursting upon the face of earth. And that light will not only expose but it will sear. It is a light, a fire that demands preparation, and so God is taking us and plowing us up at an accelerated rate to prepare us for what is to come.

Picture a field that is being plowed, versus a fallow field—a deserted, isolated uncultivated field that no one ever works. The field that is being plowed up is continually being developed; it has the constant attention of one kind or another of the husbandman, or the cultivator of the soil. In other words, my God is my husbandman, He is my Plowman. And He is continually working in the soil of my life.

But look at a fallow field. That field is manifesting a state of death. What is death? Death is simply lying there reacting in endless cycles to the seasons of a fallen earth. How many times have we simply lain around and been manipulated in endless cycles by whatever wind desires to blow? That is spiritual passivity. We lie back and allow every cold wind that wants to blow, every spirit of depression, rejection, bitterness, hurt, or isolation, to blow across our field. The fallow field and hard ground do not allow the plow of the Lord to do its work.

What happens when everything is going fairly well in your life? Say circumstances are fine. The dishwasher may clog up occasionally, but other than that, you don't have any big problems at this point in your life. You wake up one morning a little depressed. "I feel a little down today." You start thinking about how you feel down and the more you think about it, the more down you feel. Pretty soon, "Well, actually my body doesn't feel all that well today either. I have a little headache. I think I'll just stay at home today. Probably I need some rest. People haven't been very nice to me lately. I have put up with so much from people."

Before you know it, you have chosen a downward trend of crusty, fallow earth simply responding and reacting to whatever wishes to blow through your life. Soil must be more sensitive to the voice of the plow, the sound of the Word, than it is to the sticks and stones. As crust and hardness form, we become more sensitive to the voice of the enemy than we are to the voice of God.

WHOSE VOICE WOULD SPEAK IN THIS DAY?

If we could picture the voices of the enemies who speak to us, we would realize that the faces of the enemy are like whited sepulchers and their throats like open graves. Like some of those horror movies, we would realize the words are like destructive vapors, formless, void and sulfuric: NOT THE BREATH OF GOD. Not the winds of the Spirit, but other vapors, dark, violent, and full of hatred. But they are just words, empty, vain, and meaningless—words flying through the air, filling it with thick smoke, like hailstones on a dark and windless night.

And we who often walk through the hailstones—pellets driving as the rain would drive, stinging the face, pitting the scalp—we plod, head bent against the onslaught, we walk, and wonder. Not about why the pellets are there, not about what they are, not about from where they came from, but we wonder how they are going to affect the next day, the next hour, the next moment. We often even accept them as our own thoughts instead of taking them captive to the obedience of Christ.

We forget that our steps are ordered by the Holy One. Like victims, we constantly react and respond in endless cycles to the assault of death. We

19

forget that the winds and the waves obey HIS will. And the dominion and the authority that He has given us extend to the onslaught of the enemy's hail.

So rejoice in hope! The thoughts often become words and without sensitivity or discernment we find ourselves simply repeating everything that comes into our head, not even realizing where it came from.

We must recognize and understand: Where do the winds and thoughts come from? Is it the rain and wind sent to water the earth, renewing it and bringing it into Harvest? Or is it the rain and wind of destruction sent by the destroyer? Is it the tongue of the learned? the enticing words of men's wisdom? Or is it the insinuating, insidious crafty and subtle voice of the one who would lead aimless and innocent feet into rocky and steep paths leading to nowhere? Whose voice would speak in this day? Whose voice would lead, whose voice would cry? Whose voice would roar? Whose voice would whisper? If the voice of depression wants to speak into our lives, we say, "Oh, yes, I am so depressed!" Immediately we have embraced it.

But the voice of the Lord encourages us to say, "The joy of the Lord is my strength. He is my joy." Where there is light, there can be no darkness and depression is darkness. So at that point, we have a choice. Are we going to listen to the voice of the wind of depression, which is death, or are we going to allow the plow of the Lord to plow into our will and nudge it so that we say, "I don't have to deal with that dead root of depression anymore. It was crucified with Christ on Calvary. I bind you, spirit of depression in the Name of Jesus, and I take you out. I pull you out by the root and I put you out of my life. I am going to rejoice today. I will worship and praise You Lord, and allow Your Word to be my joy and my strength."

We must learn to speak the Word of God not only to others but to ourselves. We don't have to wait for a minister to pray for us. We are filled with the Spirit of the Living God. We are filled with that very Spirit that said, "Let there be light!" We have the plow of the Word of God right inside of us. What will we do? Will we choose to exercise the authority given to us not just for others but over our own life? Will we become a fruitful field and allow the plow to work or will we choose to be a hard, crusty fallow field and just respond to every wind that blows?

WEEDS, THISTLES AND THORNS

WEEDS. Crust that has formed around rocks, sticks, and hard things foreign to the soil is a perfect environment for weeds and thorns to thrive. A weed, according to the dictionary, is "any undesired, uncultivated plant that grows in profusion so as to crowd out a desired crop." Weeds are a serious irritant to the farmer because of the undesirable effect on his plants. Weeds grow profusely and determinedly choke out life. Without diligent care, weeds will take over a crop, and in a fallow field, weeds reign as king.

Not many of us actually desire the weedy, undesirable traits in our lives which choke out the seed. After all, few would argue that hatred poisons the system and steals joy, leaving in its wake misery and depression. It is also easy to see that where one "weed" has been allowed to thrive, many will join in, until soon hatred, misery, and depression have gathered with them the potential of despair, suicide, and death. Keeping soil weeded is infinitely preferable to neglecting the problems until a simple job becomes an arduous complicated and time-consuming task.

I love to grow roses. I like the way they look. I like the way they smell. But they are high maintenance plants. They get diseased and bugged easily. And most of all, they get surrounded by lots of weeds. To diligently keep out weeds, I have to watch on a daily basis, stoop, sweat and pull. But the beauty of the well-tended rose garden is more than worth it! We are like beautiful, tended and loved roses!

THISTLES. Thistles are a type of weed with thorny spikes. Known for their troublesome "pest-like" nature, they thrive particularly in grain fields. They are a definite threat because of their large downy seed balls which are scattered lavishly by the wind. They multiply rapidly and grow strong roots which resist being pulled up. Many of the problems in our lives, while multiplying rapidly, stubbornly resist the hand of the husbandman. The moment we discern a problem in our soil, let us quickly turn to our Savior, before it has taken root and developed resistance. Good soil which grows the desired seed so diligently also breeds great weeds, thistles, and thorns.

And others fell among the thorns, and the thorns came up and choked them out. Matt. 13:7

THORNS. As I began to meditate on the thorns in our lives, I found the definition of "thorn": "a woody plant bearing sharp, impeding processes; something that causes distress or irritation, full of difficulty or controversial points; to impede the progress of." Wood is symbolic of humanity. Often our very humanity propagates itself and brings on its own misery. We generate our own thorns, choosing to be thorny by providing an atmosphere where thorns can thrive. There is an innate trait in man which desires to nurse grievances, infirmity, and misery. We like to talk about them and nurture them, thereby encouraging more growth of thorns. The flesh loves to glory in itself—to be king.

Plants that have thorns often are found in harsh and untended environments. In our lives, many times resisting the attention of the husbandman is a situation propagated by outside circumstances, even before inner conflicts begin. The environment actually IS harsh. The people around have been harsh. There may have been abuse and even violence. So we intentionally allow thorns to grow as a protection. We actually will use the thorns as weapons to keep away the very people and the very things that can deliver us from the thorns. "I'll never be hurt that way again." Worry, anxiety, unbelief and skepticism are thorns which easily prick those around us with a constant goad of pain and death.

THORNS IMPEDE THE PROGRESS OF THE SEED.

Thorns, whether generated by self or inflicted, are an irritant that "impede the progress of." In harsh environments we provide ample opportunity for the growth and propagation of thorns by not allowing the blade of the Spirit to till the soil, indicating the lack of a thankful teachable heart. Thorny plants in poorly cultivated soil steal needed nutrients and space from the seed, as well as competing for vital moisture.

The only way one can get close to something thorny is to wear protection. Care must be taken around people with thorns. Just as a rose bush can surprise us with a thorn, so the thorns in people can prick us. A root of bitterness will defile others. A person prickly with bitterness is going to defile everything he touches, causing "distress and irritation." It is difficult to communicate with people in that condition, and no matter what you say or how you say it, somehow it becomes controversial. The venom and poison that spew out will inflict wounds, and often the wounded won't even know that it happened until later.

The thorns on a cactus are much like what we know as the leaves on other plants. Leaves are the life-bearing part of the plant. A thorny plant has taken the life-bearing part and made it a thorn instead, resulting in diminished growth and potential. Few cactus-like plants grow as tall as a cypress. So we can see that many of us in harsh environments take the very thing that should be a life-giving element and make it a thorn and use it as a weapon against others. In poorly cultivated soil, thorns impede the progress of the seed in both ourselves and others around us, hampering growth and life.

THORNS CAN ENCOURAGE AN ATMOSPHERE FOR REVELATION.

Thorns often inflict the GOOD soil whereby the soil joyfully reaches to the husbandman in thanks for the opportunity of further plowing and cultivation, with the result that the thorn IMPEDES THE PROGRESS OF THE FLESH to exult and glory in itself.

> And lest I should be exalted above measure by the abundance of
> the revelations, a thorn in the flesh was given to me, a messenger
> of satan to buffet me, lest I be exalted above measure.
> 2 Cor. 12:7 NKJV

When we seek with all our hearts, we will find. In the midst of the pain of thorns, the apostle Paul still found an abundance of revelation. The Greek word for "revelations" in this scripture comes from several different root words. The first, "apokalupsis," means "disclosure." As we delve into the next root, we find "apokalupto", "to take off the cover", and the last root meaning "in various senses of place or time or relation." In other words, the place of revelation is another place in God that is not bounded by time, place, or relations. There are places in God that are covered up. "It is the glory of God to conceal a matter, and it is the glory of kings to search it out" (Prov. 25:2).

The word "abundance" means "a throwing beyond others--to throw beyond the usual mark." He is preparing our new earth to bear all manner of precious fruit, in all wisdom, understanding, and glory, far beyond the usual mark. God is raising up an end-time Elijah company for the great harvest and we are a part of that end-time generation. It is an end-time prophetic generation, and we will be able to move in a place in God that is beyond our experience, intellect, knowledge, or tradition.

My hunger for those realms in God is so great that it came as a distinct shock the day the Lord revealed to me that many people actually DON'T WANT revelation. They want the non-challenging, non-threatening word that asks no commitment. "It is the glory of God to conceal a matter." God often seems to protect His glory from the carnal-minded man and then reveals it to those who truly seek with that depth of longing and yearning born in us from the very heart of the Father "Deep calls to deep at the sound of Thy waterfalls; all Thy breakers and Thy waves have rolled over me" (Psa. 42:7).

God hides Himself from that which is not elementally Himself and therefore from most of that which makes up man ("Come out from their midst and be separate" 2 Cor. 6:17). That is why the prophetic word of God, just like the written word, pierces to divide soul and spirit. Like an arrow it pierces directly to hit that part of man that is like God, transcending man's experience, doctrine, and age. The level of Word may differ greatly depending on the vessel releasing it. The container for the Presence and nature of God often varies greatly in size. If the prophet's capacity is great enough, he will release enough of God's power to transcend the lack in the person to whom he is ministering, and literally plow the furrow in them as the Word goes forth—preparing the way of the Lord.

REMOVING THORNS

The way of the Lord, riding through the deserts and shaking our very foundations with His Presence, must be prepared by removing every possible obstacle in His path. In this last day, we entreat His grace in our state of cultivation. Paul called upon the Lord, the husbandman, the giver of Life, to take the thorn.

Concerning this I entreated the Lord three times that it might depart from me. 2 Cor. 12:8

God's answer and Paul's subsequent answer to His is a powerful exhortation and example to us all in this daily inner struggle to become good soil, thirty, sixty, and a hundred-fold.

And He has said to me, "My grace is sufficient for you, for power is perfected in weakness." Most gladly, therefore, I will rather boast about my weaknesses, that the power of Christ may dwell in me. 2 Cor 12:9

Paul says, "I will glory in my infirmities." Many of us have been carefully taught to hide all of our weaknesses. We never speak about them. Instead of confessing our faults that we may be healed, or boasting in our weaknesses like Paul, we ignore the situation completely, even "confessing" vehemently to the contrary. The literal meaning of the Greek word for infirmities is "feebleness of body or mind, frailty or malady." The root word means "strengthless." His strength is perfected in our weakness. Literally, if we use OUR strength, it fights for position with His. But if we have none, His mighty power has free reign in us. So we will boast about our strengthlessness, because the strength of God and His miraculous power is complete in us. "Most gladly therefore" means "with great pleasure, sweetly, with sensual delight." With the sweetness of His nature, I will brag on the power of the Anointed One who rests within me.

If thorns go into unrepentant flesh and stay there, the angry flesh will get red, swollen, and very, very sensitive. Eventually it will get infected, poisonous and full of pus— "offended." It is an intruder that can ultimately poison the whole system. And healing has to come from within. What we desire is that God take the thorn out, but what God wants us to do is simply to become like Him. The triumph of the thorns is that the sicker you are, the more desperate you become to find the doctor, and the best one around regardless of the price. So the result of the thorns, as we begin to glory and boast in the Lord and in His miraculous and mighty power, is that we will seek Him more desperately than we ever did when we were doing so well.

"Rejoice always, again I say, rejoice!" The joy of the Lord is our strength, and as we are changed from glory to glory, the healthy flesh (soil) will send fresh blood to the offended area, promoting healing. As I lay in the hospital recovering from third-degree burns, the doctors had taken large sheets of skin from the tops of my thighs and calves to replace the destroyed skin of my face, hands and ears. Then to promote the growth of new skin on my legs, they had placed thin strips of gauze on the raw flesh. The gauze, acting as a surrogate skin, quickly grew attached to the flesh. One day they decided that it would be best to strip off the gauze. Thus ensued a horrifying period of totally unnecessary agony, as I was literally "skinned alive"-- again. The truth that was hidden from the decision-maker was that as the skin renewed itself underneath the gauze, it would simply push the gauze off, much as it pushes off a scab when it is no longer necessary. Great agony and additional scarring resulted when they stripped it off AHEAD OF TIME. In like manner, instead of "pulling weeds" we plant healthy seed, which eventually crowds out the weeds and thorns.

> Then the Lord answered me and said: "Write the vision and make it plain on tablets, that he may run who reads it. For the vision is yet for an appointed time; but at the end it will speak, and it will not lie. Though it tarries, wait for it; because it will surely come, it will not tarry." Hab.2:2-3

Our times are in His hands, the hands of a faithful and wise husbandman, who knows the seasons and those things appointed for each. How many visions have been aborted, sabotaged, and destroyed because of precipitate action by zealous, well-meaning saints "doing the work of the ministry"? The seeds of the Lord must develop according to His wisdom and the uprooting as well. In His timing and in His way, He will plow our ground, remove the stones, roots, weeds, thistles and thorns. As we submit to His care, we become good soil, yielding fruit for our Master—in due season.

> But others fell into good ground, and brought forth fruit, some a hundredfold, some sixtyfold, some thirtyfold. Who has ears to hear, let him hear. Matt. 13:8-9 NKJV

Five-fold ministries all across the face of the earth are hurting, getting hit with everything you can imagine: thorns like hail stones are hitting them from the enemy. Why is it happening? Because they are part of an end-time generation that will display the miraculous power of God. But as we trust in the One Who made us, we allow His timetable its freedom in our lives. We, as all good soil should, look eagerly toward the attention of a faithful husbandman to manifest His ways. We sharpen our ears that we might HEAR what the Spirit would say to the church. We watch with anticipation the approach of the sharp plow, and we recognize that we are simply the clay, and it is HE who is the potter, the farmer, the plowman, the husbandman, the One Who loves us best. And we are thankful. The key to this dance of Life is not to focus on the thorns—but to constantly be thankful for His goodness, His grace, and His care.

II

THE PLOW

"Behold, the days are coming," saith the Lord, "when the plowman shall overtake the reaper, and the treader of grapes him who sows seed; and the mountains shall drip with sweet wine, and all the hills shall flow with it." Amos 9:13 NKJV

Central thought: The plowman shall overtake the reaper. I may come bearing seed, but you will stand right next to me reaping a harvest and next to you one will be baking bread, and another breaking that bread and taking it to the nations. No one job is more important than the other. We are all working together at the same time for the same purpose, united in the indescribable wonder of His Presence. The Lord in this day is causing the mountains, the new earth, to drip with sweet wine. The sweetness and the joy, the freshness of the Lord is our strength.

THE PLOW

There is an appointed time for everything. And there is a time for every event under heaven—a time to give birth, and a time to die; a time to plant, and a time to uproot what is planted. Eccl. 3:1-2

Before we can sink our teeth into juicy red apples or smell freshly baked bread made from golden fields of grain or taste steamy buttered potatoes newly pulled from the garden, before we can experience all of the benefits of a fruitful soil, the earth must be broken into and violently turned upside down with a sharp, business-like looking tool called a PLOW. Plowing is necessary for planting, sowing, and harvest.

WHAT AND WHY IS THE PLOW?

The dictionary definition of the word "to plow" is "to break, cut into, or dig up the earth." When we examine the common instrument used across the world for centuries, we see a sharp sturdy blade, the part which goes beneath the surface of the earth, and handles made of wood. Just as this blade dips and cuts into natural earth, so there is a sharp two-edged blade or sword, the Word of God, piercing to the dividing line of soul and spirit, deep in our inner "earth." Generally, in the Word, wood signifies humanity or an earthen vessel. Much like the natural handles on a plow, human nature often tries to control what the Word of God can do and where it can go. Our carnal nature, particularly our mind, is at enmity against all that God wants to do in our lives (Rom. 8:7). We desire to "be in control" at all times. We joke about "getting a handle on things." And then we proceed to do just that. We are most secure when we are most in control of all that touches us or ours.

It is interesting to note that as the plowman applies pressure to the old-fashioned wooden handles of his plow, the blade cuts deeper into the earth, and as he releases the pressure from the handles, the blade rises up out of the earth. As we truly desire the workings of God in our lives, we allow pressure to come to bear upon our carnality and our selfish ways, and His plow dips deeper into our inner man. But if we allow our will full sway and control, the plow of the Lord will lift from our life, and vital cleansing may go undone. Maintenance of our field will take longer and require re-plowing at a later date.

In the days when there was nothing but the plowman and the plow itself, what was done had to be done totally in the physical strength of the lone and exhausted farmer. But as the process developed, he used some other kind of energy force (oxen or horses and then gas power), with the obvious advantage of getting more done faster and more efficiently. So we, in our walk with Him, become infinitely more fruitful and valuable to His kingdom, whether beginning as new converts or continuing on in maturity, by allowing His power and spirit to fuel our activities instead of our inadequate, narrow and limited carnal mind operating alone.

> Therefore, on account of you, Zion will be plowed as a field. For from Zion will go forth the law, even the word of the Lord from Jerusalem. Micah 3:12,4:2

The process of being plowed is not an option, just as natural plowing was never an option if one wanted to eat. We are commanded to plow, to break up the fallow, hard ground of our hearts, that place where He now writes His laws and commands His sacrifices. For the old is being plowed under to make way for the manifestation of the new, and out of the midst of that which is plowed shall go forth the Word of the Lord.

> Sow to yourselves in righteousness, reap in mercy; break up your fallow ground: for it is time to seek the Lord, till He come and rain righteousness upon you. Hosea 10:12

Break it up, break it up. Have you ever said, "Oh, God, have mercy!" God IS mercy and He is in us. The only thing to keep us from reaping mercy is fallow ground. So we break up that fallow ground and then as we seek the Lord, He rains living water into and through us: the waters of righteousness and mercy.

Pioneers in the old American West experienced an urgency about getting the plowing done and the earth prepared to bring forth fruit. The plowing of our inner earth is no less urgent. The plowing of the nations even more so. The Lord of the Harvest is preparing the former and latter rains with world-wide harvest in mind. It is TIME to seek the Lord, that He release His life-giving rains upon dry and thirsty ground prepared to receive. The more we give up our control to the Lord, the more he can accomplish in and through us. The more we partner with Him in the nations in this process, the closer we come to world-wide harvest.

THE PLOW DIGS

Exactly what does the plow do? Digs—digs—digs—digs. And when the plow turns up, it turns over. Does your life feel upside-down? Do you feel cut, lacerated, and pierced? The Spirit of God is moving in our hearts and He is cutting beneath the surface, turning over and exposing. He is rooting up, digging out and plucking up. There is the time to pluck up and there is the time to plant. We must allow these times of the Lord. Yes, it hurts. Any kind of sword or plow will hurt when it pierces the soil of our lives. But this necessary digging or breaking of the earth will turn over and expose the hidden things both good and bad: the dead roots, the sticks, the stones. These things must be removed, along with old tree stumps and reminders of old plantings that are dead and fruitless, having become obstacles to the growth of new life.

> Go through, go through the gates; clear the way for the people; build up, build up the highway; Remove the stones, lift up a standard over the peoples. Isa. 62:10

Some of us have roots of rejection, bitterness, or wounded spirits still embedded in our flesh—in our mind, our emotions, or our memory. All of these things are dead—the old nature, the old man—and should be put away. So that sharp, two-edged sword of the plow, the plow of the Word which pierces to the dividing line of soul and spirit, that blade is going down into the soil to turn up all the stones, the old dead obstacles to life, so that they can be thrown away forever. The blood of Jesus is all powerful and when we are filled, saturated and covered with the blood of Jesus, we will allow the plow of God freedom to take care of those things which must be removed. It will bring the things which are hidden to the top and then the Spirit of God will remove the heavy burden of excess weight and set us free. So much has begun when we are born again, but it continues throughout our lives as we continue to walk in the spirit.

> A new heart also will I give you, and a new spirit will I put within you: and I will take away the stony heart out of your flesh, and I will give you a heart of flesh. Eze. 36:26

Soil that is heavy with stones, roots, and dead things is hard and resistant to the turning over and airing out brought by the plow. It is much like excess baggage in a huge airplane. Sometimes when I am flying across the great waters, I know what I have in my suitcase and I see all the other hundreds of people on the plane and I know they have at least that much in theirs. Going down the runway for takeoff is a challenge when you are thinking that only by the grace of God will the plane get off the ground! Not only must it get off the ground, but it must rise to thirty-six thousand feet or more and fly. When you are crossing the Atlantic Ocean or the Pacific, or the Indian Ocean or the China Sea, you are interested not only in getting the plane up, but you're interested in keeping it up. Sometimes you feel, "If only I hadn't bought that extra suitcase! If I could just lighten this load a little!" God is in the process of lightening our load and getting us ready, not just in crises times, but for permanent, daily fruitfulness. He is getting out the great plow of God and breaking up the fallow soil in order to remove useless, excess baggage.

And so the plow moves aside and changes the look of things. We think we know who we are. That is the big thing in the world. Find yourself. To thine own self be true. So the big push is to find out who you are and then flaunt it. We like to say, "Oh, I am like this," or "Oh, I am just not like that," because it gives us comfort—the known is always more palatable than the unknown. How we hold on to the things we think we know! And God wants us to hold onto Him instead! Every now and then I will complain, "I don't know who I am anymore!" And the Lord will reply, "Good! Now I can use you!"

With God you are always in such a state of change that you can't pin down "who you really are." Just about the time you get comfortable, another layer sloughs off and then another and another. All of our protective coverings, our masks which carefully and effectively hide us from one another, are broken up and turned under by the great Plow. Then many layers later, there is God! And really, who we are is that we are like God, because we are being changed into His image.

In the stress and business of public life and often in ministry, we begin to lose sight of Who He is and Whose we are. We use phrases such as "my gifting, my anointing, my ministry." It is not anyone's ministry but HIS, which is the whole point. It must change according to the task at hand. The great apostle Paul says, "To the weak I became weak, that I might win the weak; I have become all things to all men, that I may by all means save some" (1 Cor. 9:22). We must forget about our "image" long enough for God to get a word in edgewise!

In digging, sometimes things come to the surface that shock even ourselves by their presence. We may even strike reservoirs of contaminated water which defile the soil. There may be old cesspools and dumping grounds of many unsavory things that have been long forgotten. Many of us, instead of allowing the dealings of God in our lives, simply seal off cesspools of hurt, bitterness, and grief, leaving the site to contaminate even generations of relationships. Do we need a gusher of contaminated, poisoned water to burst out into a joyful scene of harvest?? No! But instead, the soil will be homogenized and mixed by a merciful and wise plowman. Then the cesspool, broken up and mixed into the earth, serves as fertilizer, much like the crust, producing the kind of good soil that will joyfully receive the seed.

Even as we are turned upside down and remixed, the plow aerates the soil, blending it with the wind and breath of life, preserving the moisture, the living water, and making the earth consistent with itself. Many of us are up and down: spiritual yo-yos, depending on where our emotions are on any given day. But the Eternal Father never changes; He is the same yesterday, today, and forever. And so shall we be. Like Him, not like ourselves; reproducing after HIS image, not after our own (Gen. 5:3).

DIGGING REVEALS HIDDEN WEALTH

When the plow goes into the earth, furrows are dug. Of course, the primary reason for plowing is to prepare the soil to receive the seed. We will explore this in depth over the next chapters. Plowing or digging for the purpose of planting seed usually involves relatively shallow digging. But as we allow the blade to penetrate more deeply into the earth, one finds oil wells, gold mines, or even water wells, depending upon the depth reached. With expensive machinery designed for digging deep into the earth, veins of richness can be tapped, producing power and energy for millions of people. Let's digress a moment from plowing in order to plant, and explore deeper digging.

OIL WELLS. The world needs the oil of the Holy Spirit. It needs the anointing of a gusher. We must allow the drilling of the Lord in our lives to hit the mother lode. I am ready for that oil not to have to be pumped and pumped; I am ready for a GUSHER. I don't want a little drip; I want the thousand-barrels-a-day kind! The anointing breaks the yokes of bondage and every one of us has that anointing within us. Many just don't know how to release it or let it out. That is what God is teaching us with the great sword of the Spirit. As He digs and drills deep into our being, He opens the fountains of the deep and calls them forth out of our midst (Gen. 7:11). The rivers of anointing that flow so freely in the lives of those we so admire in God are resident within all of us, simply awaiting release.

GOLD MINES. Many times the hardest digging, often literally a chipping away at rock, produces the richest prize. Out of mountains of rock come gold mines, precious substances used the world over "for glory and for beauty" (Ex.28:2). Gold speaks of deity, of kingliness, of purification by fire. Our inner man, strengthened with His mighty power, is being transformed from glory to glory into the same substance as that of our Maker. We must receive the revelation of who we really are. We are heirs according to the promise. We are sons of the Living God. We are the Bride of Christ. Jesus is our Bridegroom. We are one with Him. Until we have a revelation of that, we will still operate up on the surface, up above all that crust and all the while, down underneath the sticks and stones, lies all the gold of Christ in us, the hope of glory.

WATER WELLS. As the children of Israel wandered all those long years ago through the dry and dusty wilderness, the richest find of all digging was that which produced life-giving water. Wars were fought and long-lasting feuds established over lands where water wells had been dug. Lands with springs of water and fresh-water lakes were hotly contested and bitterly coveted. In lands of such intense heat, even wells dried up in the summer, making water the most precious of all commodities. Isaac, the son of God's promise, was one of the most active well-diggers of ancient times. It is an interesting testament to their importance that wells, like altars, were accorded names and referred to as such.

Then Isaac dug again the wells of water which had been dug in the days of his father Abraham, for the Philistines had stopped them up after the death of Abraham; and he gave them the same names which his father had given them. Gen. 26:18

The Philistines were always enemies of the sons of promise, of God's children. The Hebrew word "Philistine" means "migratory or rolling in the dust, roll or wallow, self." Philistines are indicative of the fleshly, carnal nature which is always at enmity with the ways and purposes of God. They stopped up the precious wells of Abraham, dug with such sacrifice and maintained with much devotion. But the son of promise was about his father's business! The loving husbandman will always dig after that priceless treasure so valued by the Father. The wells of living water in us are being dug and valued with a new name, known only to Him (Rev.2:17).

It is interesting to note that watchmen were not only set upon the walls of the cities, but also put in the fields and at the wells, to guard the living substance from enemies who would destroy the life of the living. "Thou art my hiding place; Thou dost preserve me from trouble; Thou dost surround me with songs of deliverance. Selah" (Psa.32:7). When we hide ourselves in Him, guarding our hearts with all diligence under the shelter of His wing, digging, plowing, planting, and harvest all go forth under His watchful care, and songs of deliverance fill the air even in the darkness. Hidden in Him, digging down to the precious substance within can be a joyous experience.

You are a garden spring, a well of fresh water, and streams flowing from Lebanon. Song 4:15

But whoever drinks of the water that I shall give him shall never thirst; but the water that I shall give him shall become in him a well of water springing up to eternal life. John 4:14

OLD AND NEW WELLS

O Lord, I give to you all the wells in my life. I consecrate them and offer them up on the altar of my self-will. That you will take, please, the old wells, dug for the wrong reasons in the wrong places with the wrong tools, and fill them in—pack them Lord, with Your substance, with Your seed, with Your wisdom, and with Your healing. That the cracked and dry earth would become one again with that meant for it, and Divine Purpose would moisten the hard walls and make the sight a useful place for the plow.

Take, Lord, the old wells that You Yourself have dug, and continue to perfect, to hollow out, to plunge ever deeper, that the living waters which flow will be artesian in nature, not generated by sweat and effort, but by Your grace. Let these waters bring life and healing and joy. And Lord, I offer eagerly new well sights, looking earnestly for Your Hand, for Your sharp instruments busily at work in the soil of my life. Dig, Lord, dig, and dig. Make the container deep and wide and big. Make it big enough for Yourself Lord—for all of Yourself and the new creature you have created me to be.

JUDAH SHALL PLOW

PRAISE. The Bible tells us that "Judah shall plow" (Hosea 10:11). The Hebrew word, "Judah," means "praise." Our God inhabits the praises of His people, and as we praise and worship in and through Him, our hearts are plowed and prepared to receive the Word as it is taught and sown in the Body of Christ. To live in God's presence is to be plowed. We enter His gates with thanksgiving and His courts with praise, and in giving thanks to Him, we bless His name (Psa. 100:4).

In our corporate worship services, a new freedom and spirit of rejoicing is bringing great release to hearts burdened with the cares of life. Many come together to worship with hearts hardened from recent strife, confusion, or despair. As New Covenant priests minister to the Living God, praise plows the untilled soil, renewing its softness and fruitfulness, preparing the way for the preaching of the Seed of the Word.

"A merry heart doeth good like a medicine: but a broken spirit drieth the bones" (Prov. 17:22). The word for "broken" in Hebrew is "naka," meaning "smitten, afflicted, broken, wounded" and comes from a root word meaning "to smite or drive away." Praise and thanksgiving bring life; afflicted and wounded spirits drive away life. He IS the Life, and it is only in His Presence, beholding and worshipping Him in all joy, that we are changed from glory to glory, growing even more into His image, into that Divine Seed.

Repentance is a key in these last days of renewal when even the elite will be deceived. Repent means "to think differently or afterwards, reconsider." Opinions and traditions of the mind of man are running rampant, spurred on by a society consumed with humanism and human-worship. Our opinions cause a hardness in us to the Word of God, literally making it null and void in our lives. Living in repentance is a joy, not an onerous duty. A pastor once told me with great enthusiasm, "I love to repent! I do it all the time!" It was the first time that I saw repentance as a joyous release from harsh emotions and wrong mind-sets, a refreshing that leads to new life (Acts 3:19).

> See to it that no one takes you captive through philosophy and
> empty deception, according to the tradition of men, according to
> the elementary principles of the world, rather than according to
> Christ. Col. 2:8

CORPORATE WORSHIP. As we let go of what we think we know and allow the plow of God to do its work in praise, familiar programs and patterns which are so comforting to leaders in churches today are swept away by the whirlwinds of His glory. The presence of the Lord comes as His leaders repent, submit to the plow, and allow His winds to blow in the service to carry the seed. What is the purpose of a corporate worship service?

This is a challenge in today's services of carefully organized agenda. Once the ground (service, hearts) have been plowed in praise, where do we go from there? Insensitivity to the Spirit can trample and destroy the carefully prepared ground, the atmosphere of releasing Presence. We must allow the Spirit to continue to carry us in His desired purpose even though other things may have been planned. Holy Spirit can be gloriously spontaneous, by-passing carnal thinking and leading the people of the Lord to deeper and deeper Presence and intimacy with Him.

So often in our worship services, we have learned how to praise the Lord, following the guidelines of the Word in shouting unto God, dancing before Him, clapping and singing with all of our might. But intimacy with our Beloved can be even more difficult for us than it often is in our relationships with one another. We understand definite directives, but what do we do with the God Who has inhabited those very praises and enters our experience with His person?

> And when they had made an end of offering, the king and all that were present with him BOWED THEMSELVES, AND WORSHIPPED. 2 Chron. 29:29

Response to the Presence of the Almighty in the Word was usually marked by falling to the ground or bowing—not requesting, declaring, preparing, or warring. Plowing, or praise, endures for a season, but when the soil is properly prepared, the farmer moves on to the next step.

> Does the farmer plow continually to plant seed? Does he continually turn and harrow the ground? Does he not level its surface, and sow? For his God instructs and teaches him properly. Isa. 28:24-26

Over-plowing will produce furrows too deep for the seed, even making ditches and ruts that would hold too much moisture and rot the seed destined for life. Response to the Presence of the Living God demands faithfulness, worship, and obedience. Even as Isaiah's body fell to the ground at the Presence of the Lord of Hosts, so our flesh must fall before Him and allow His Spirit to move as it will as we worship. When the Spirit of the Lord has plowed hearts in praise, inhabited those praises, and His winds blow strongly, THEREIN lies our greatest challenge: to follow where He goes deeper in worship. We have then entered a new realm. Let us learn together the move of God, and leave tradition and old comfortable ruts behind. There may not be a signpost other than the Word of God which exhorts us to lean not to our own understanding but in ALL our ways acknowledge Him and HE WILL DIRECT OUR PATH.

I am the type of person who wants to know everything yesterday. I must not only know it, I must understand it. I want to know everything about everything. Why did this happen? Why did that happen? I want a blueprint that has definite and detailed instructions with clear timelines. I was always a curious child. I was the type that drove my mother wild with questions, questions, questions. You know when the child gets to the question stage? Many of us have carried that trait into the sanctuary along with our opinions and the program. If the wind of the Spirit doesn't blow according to our map, we stop the ship dead in the water.

I had a most significant dream several years ago. This dream was so full of the love of the Lord that I didn't want to wake up. He embraced me and then picked me up and began carrying me. Of course, I immediately assumed we were going somewhere. My next thought was, "Where are we going?" Here I am being carried by the Lord of Glory, and I occupy myself looking over His arm attempting to see the ground go by (where is He taking me?). So I said, "Lord, where are you carrying me?" There was a long silence. All too many of us are familiar with the silences of God. Then the Lord said, "Are you ready for the end times?" And I woke up.

The story of my life!!! Of course, since He answered me with a question, I spent quite a period of time trying to figure out what He meant. Basically, He is carrying us all and we are going somewhere. Most of us are trying to jump out of His arms and help Him. Once He begins to move in our lives or in our services, it is such a relief that He is moving, but we are never satisfied. We always want to go faster. We always want to go further. And most important of all, we want to orchestrate it all. We analyze each moment in our services, sifting, judging, choosing and discarding. Certainly, God desires to maintain "decency and order" in the midst of the blowing of His winds. Let us just make sure it is indeed HIS order, and not our own.

As leadership in the Body of Christ struggles to analyze the current winds, often we find competitive viewpoints and traditions vying with one another. Competition between the pieces of the Body is ridiculous, the toe fighting against the hand, the nose against the arm. We must realize that we are all, indeed, on the same side—on God's side. If one day I can wield the plow of the Lord in your life, one day you may wield it in mine. We may all speak at different times and different seasons into one another's lives because it is only together that we form the whole council of God.

No one person has the whole mind of the Lord. No one denomination or one church has the whole picture; each has been given a piece. The plowman shall overtake the reaper. I may come bearing seed, but you will stand right next to me reaping a harvest and next to you one will be baking bread, and another breaking that bread and taking it to the nations. No one job is more important than the other. We are all working together at the same time for the same purpose, united in the indescribable wonder of His Presence. The Lord in this day is causing the mountains, the new earth, to drip with sweet wine. The sweetness and the joy, the freshness of the Lord is our strength.

So the ministry of restoration will cause us to explore together the fresh new improved methods of plowing, planting, and reaping. Refusing to be teachable and open to fresh winds of God will only result in hard ground, small crops, disease and pestilence. In other words, scattering seed (much preaching of the Word) upon ground not properly prepared (little praise) will result in loss of crops and lack of food. So we maintain an attitude of repentance, we plow in praise, humble ourselves in worship, and allow God to properly (according to HIS order and purposes) prepare that particular ground for the seeding of the Word. We will allow intimacy to come in our individual lives and also in the corporate church life. Harvest and revival will come. Will we reject the unfamiliar as God's glory begins to manifest?

LEAVING THE PLOW TO GO TO WAR

> Proclaim ye this among the Gentiles; Prepare war, wake up the mighty men, let all the men of war draw near; let them come up: beat your plowshares into swords and your pruning hooks into spears: let the weak say, I am strong. Joel 3:9-10

There is a strong move today in the Body of Christ to exchange the praises of God from time to time, both individually and corporately, for the tools of war. Fresh perspective and revelation has burst upon the horizon regarding the strongholds and principalities of the enemy, giving rise, as "new" moves always do, to controversy. Are we burying our heads in the sand and opening our flank to attack by ignoring the devil? Are we venerating the devil by giving him too much attention? Are we actually putting faith in his power by feeling we have to bind it so much? Is no news of the devil and his activities good news, or is no news ignorance which could lead to ambush?

Some worship services omit or dilute worship and become battlegrounds as shouts and claps and stomps of war "bind spirits" and "bring down strongholds." In our passage from Joel, the phrase "Prepare war" actually translates "Sanctify by sacrifice and proper rites." And so we find, as in most moves of God taken up by man, that the Truth of God often lies somewhere in between both sides of the controversy. All power HAS been given the believer to tread upon serpents and scorpions and all manner of evil. Being transformed into His image, we literally enact the Word of God, much as the prophets of old. So in each service, is it our idea or plan, or which direction is the spirit actually leading us? Sometimes war, yes, more often worship, or prophetic flow. But our way of warring and the Lord's plan may be very different!

The testimony of Jesus is the spirit of prophecy (Rev. 19:10), and as we plow in praise, testifying of His Name, the spirit or mantle of prophecy falls among the congregation, giving rise to a moving in the Spirit which man often finds intimidating, hard to orchestrate and impossible to control. Gifts of the Spirit flow today in many creative ways, through music and dance and spoken word, manifesting the Word and Will of the Lord in earth as it is in Heaven. Words of knowledge (1 Cor. 12:8), can reveal strategies of the enemy as the things which are hidden are shouted from the rooftops. Routing the enemy from his hiding place tends to excite emotions and stir some to react in perhaps uninhibited ways. Religious spirits, intellectual spirits, and all inhibited humans HATE IT and immediately try to orchestrate, control or obliterate it. Instead of venting our disgust, fear, disapproval, skepticism, distrust, etc., of one another, let us go to the Lord of Glory for the "battle plan" He has in mind for us and our particular church and situation.

Jehoshaphat, a Godly king of the tribe of Judah, always sought God before going into battle. Once, at the Lord's direction, he sent singers out before the army—whose praises confounded and defeated the enemy (11 Chron. 20:21-22). The battle is the Lord's, and it is His mighty power shed abroad in our hearts which resolves any conflict. When the arm of flesh reaches out to aid God's mighty right arm, He could withdraw His involvement to allow us to continue to "do our thing."

In the old days, the farmer had to protect his farm from attack by leaving the plow in the field to go to war, or there would be nothing left in that field to bring to harvest. But if he left the field too long, freshly plowed furrows became hard and brittle in the sun, washed away and filled with water in the rain. Then plowing had to be done over before seed could be sown. There is a time for battle, and a time to return from battle.

Today in our worship services, great power is released in the praises of His people, and corporate anointing can do mighty exploits as unified troops send great shouts of light into the darkness. As we stay sensitive to the leading of the Spirit in the midst of warring intercession, we find that He will guide us back into worship, back to the field, before sight is lost of the original goal: planting and harvest. Too many times, "praise warfare" can become a runaway steed going nowhere rather than a horse among Pharaoh's chariots (Song 1:9) and a lover of the King.

LEAVING WAR FOR THE PLOW

> And many people shall go and say, Come ye, and let us go up to the mountain of the Lord, to the house of the God of Jacob. and they shall beat their swords into plowshares, and their spears into pruning hooks: nation shall not lift up sword against nation, neither shall they learn war any more. Isa. 2:3-5

Leaving war for the plow is just as vital a truth as leaving the plow to go to war. Both are necessary for growth, protection, and progression toward maturity. Following the flow of the Spirit in times of transition in our worship services can be a challenge. The ability to change always comes hard to us, and to become eminently adaptable must be a priority for anyone in service to the King. Walking in HIS light is certainly not always walking in the way WE would do it, think we can, or wish He would do it. His ways are not our ways, and His thoughts are not our thoughts. Therefore, becoming comfortable should be a warning sign that the cloud is about to move, many times back to the plow and on to worship and the sowing of the seed.

David's band of "mighty men" who went with him into battle were men who had understanding of the times, to know what Israel should do (1 Chron. 12:32). Any good farmer understands the seasons, recognizing the signs and sensing the changing times. As the Body of Christ has progressed toward union and maturity, music and praise has reflected that progression.

In the 1970's lively worshippers were singing, "It's Bubbling" and "Joy is the Flag." It was a sort of new or "puppy" love, a honeymoon type of love as worshippers reveled in sensations caused and released by His Presence. In the 1980's praise progressed into "Blessed Be the Lord Who Teaches My Hands to War," generally expressing love as it blessed ourselves and gave directives of action and activity. By the 1990's, praise became characterized by songs such as "Almighty God, Holy Lord." As a new age opened, attention and love began to be centered upon the Lord as our Bridegroom and union with Him, rather than on self and benefits experienced and received.

As revelation and maturity and fullness increase, praise tends to begin where worship services ended the decade before. It is important to realize the difference between style and anointing, as today's music changes again. What songs release His presence? What music leads into the depth of His glory? What leads the people from outside the camp into the most holy place? What reveals and draws us to our heavenly Bridegroom?

As leadership across the world endeavors to "write the vision," indeed, even identify that there IS a vision, strife and confusion within the ranks threatens to break the furrows and spoil the seed bed. Change can bring confusion, with some holding to old ways and others pressing on, leaving a situation of two kinds of seed, often competing and slowing the progression of harvest.

Thou shalt not sow thy vineyard with two kinds of seed, lest the whole fruit be forfeited, the seed which thou hast sown, and the increase of the vineyard. Thou shalt not plow with an ox and an ass together. Deut. 22:9-10

The Plow

Coming together as human beings, we must lay down our own opinions, dreams, and ideals, certainly our own "kingdoms," and allow the Lord God to write the vision and focus for each local church or ministry. Then it is each leader's responsibility to align himself with that vision. Unity in vision and the carrying out of the vision, both in worship services and in the sowing of the Word, will release the power and presence of Christ and reveal His purposes and plans.

> Behold, how good and how pleasant it is for brethren to dwell together in unity! It is like the precious ointment upon the head, that ran down upon the beard, even Aaron's beard: that went down to the skirts of his garments;

> As the dew of Hermon, and as the dew that descended upon the mountains of Zion: for there the Lord commanded the blessing, even life for evermore.

> Behold, bless ye the Lord, all ye servants of the Lord, which by night stand in the house of the Lord. Lift up your hands in the sanctuary, and bless the Lord. Psa. 133:1-3; 134:1-2

As believers come together releasing life in praise and worship, releasing gifts of the Spirit and prophetic flow, amazing things happen. When they were ALL TOGETHER IN ONE ACCORD, there was a sound of a mighty rushing wind, and fire came (Acts 2:1-2). When they were unanimous, having one mind and purpose, harmony led to action. God always has a purpose; He always goes somewhere. He is calling us up and growing us up, to unity not discord. He is LEADING us, let us follow!

So let's submit to the plowing and tilling of our soil, both corporately and individually, leaning always toward the prize of the glory of His Presence, eagerly awaiting that discipline that displays His love (Prov. 13:24), the cutting of the blade that signals His care, and the upheaval which always precedes the planting of the Lord. And as we travel the fields of the world, let's wield the plow with wisdom as to the times, fields, and season.

III

THE BREAKING OF THE EARTH

This is My body, which is broken for you. 1 Cor. 11:24

Central thought: It was not until Jesus broke the bread that the eyes of those who loved Him were opened and they recognized Him. As we are broken like bread to feed the hungry, the eyes of the nations will be opened, and they will see Jesus. He can only shine through broken vessels. The breaking and plowing of the soil of our lives allows the divine Seed to burst forth and shine with the blinding Light and Glory of Restored Creation. The triumph of the fruitful Garden is the inheritance and joy of the heart of a loving Plowman.

BREAKING AND SHAKING

Upheaval, turning, churning, piercing, cutting—all of us who are born again and enter the realm of the spirit have experienced the great plow of the Lord. Breaking. So many sermon topics center on the broken and contrite heart, the brokenness of the self-life. It is not a study new to most. But it is a subject resisted by many, and truly understood by few.

There is a great shaking in the earth in these last days at the eminent coming of the Lord. "Mountains quake because of Him, and the hills dissolve; indeed the earth is upheaved by His presence, the world and all the inhabitants in it" (Nah. 1:5). Pressure builds within the earth as fires heat and the earth begins to shake. When we are shaken ("I will shake the

47

heavens and the earth"), and don't allow the plow of God to work in the hard yet teeming ground, the build-up of inner pressure will seek release in destructive ways. If the plow is resisted and pressure within the earth gets too great, breaking will burst forth from within the earth with great destruction and devastation. Volcanic activity is uncontrollable with a power frightening to man. Deep fissures and crevices not fit for the seed will become pits for stagnant water and debris.

Emotions torn and damaged with tension and strife become entangled with wills not daily submitted to the disciplines of God. The mind becomes the battleground for the world, the flesh and the devil. Pressure within mounts moment by moment. Finally, without the plow of the Lord, pressure can be released in explosions of rage, violence, frustration, and anxiety. "Wretched man that I am! Who will set me free from the body of this death" (Rom. 7:24)?

This is a day when the breaking of the earth is not an option, but a necessary process of survival. This is a day for cultivation, to receive attention from a wise and loving husbandman. It is a day of preparation. It is a day to fall upon the rock, that the breaking in our lives be of His plan and purpose and order.

And whosoever shall fall on this stone shall be broken: but on whomsoever it shall fall, it will grind him to powder. Matt. 21:44

We must literally throw ourselves on the Rock. Once when I was first baptized in the Spirit, I had a vision. I saw myself in the midst of a storm surrounded by nothing but ocean. There was one huge rock that rose up out of the angry and violent sea, and I was hanging desperately onto the rock. My hair was plastered against my face with the rain and the waves, and it was evident that my strength was all but gone. The vision ended there, and I didn't understand it for a long time.

Finally, I realized that I had fallen on the rock and although I was surrounded by storm and waves and wind and rain, the rock was my place of safety. And there would come a time when I would no longer be hanging onto the rock beaten and pummeled by storms, but standing with my feet firmly planted on the Rock, which is Jesus (Psa.40:2). That Rock, Jesus, walked this earth, the Son of the Living God, in a body made of clay. His treasure, like ours, was for a time encased in an earthen vessel. And Jesus said, "This is My body, which is broken for you" (1 Cor. 11:24).

We know that in the Garden of Gethsemane, the intensity of Jesus' prayer caused His sweat to be as drops of blood falling upon the ground (Luke 22:44). In the Sanhedrin, the scornful battering broke blood vessels and skin. The legionnaires used a whip with small balls of lead to scourge and cut the skin until it was an unrecognizable mass of torn, bleeding tissue. The crown of thorns pressed into His scalp causing blood to run down into His eyes. The rough wood of the cross gouged more tears and rips into His already lacerated body. The nails driven into His flesh not only caused holes and rips, but crushed and affected nerves running all the way from His wrists up His arms, and from His feet up through His back. Finally, the sword through the pericardium into His heart broke the surrounding sac of watery fluid and released blood which flowed out with the water.

Just as it was necessary for Jesus' body to be broken that His kingdom might come, so it is necessary for His BODY, for the BODY OF CHRIST, that corporate BODY of earthen vessels enduring until He comes, be broken that His kingdom might come IN US. Although we may not endure the physical crucifixion of our Savior, we indeed must, as Paul was, be crucified WITH Him, bearing our cross daily, following in His footsteps.

> I **have been** crucified with Christ; and it is no longer I who live, but Christ lives in me; and the life which I now live in the flesh I live by faith in the Son of God, who loved me, and delivered Himself up for me. Gal. 2:20

> For if we **have become** united with Him in the likeness of His death, certainly we shall be also in the likeness of His resurrection, knowing this, that our old self was crucified with Him, that our body of sin might be done away with, that we should no longer be slaves to sin; for he who has died is freed from sin. Rom. 6:5-7

Many times, we look at the breaking of the earth, our physical or carnal earth, as a mutilation or death. If we have no vision or perspective of the triumph of the resurrection, crucifixion is unbearable. When the carnal man looks at the death of the body, in all of its various traumatic forms, it becomes an unbearable thought. I grew up with a terrible fear of death. Being a country girl, the funerals which I had to attend were sometimes frightening. The casket was always open, with the usual remarks of those passing identifying how natural or how unnatural the dead body looked, whether they should have worn their glasses or not, whether their lips looked puffy or whether they had on the right clothes. I grew up with a terrible fear of being shut up in the cold darkness of the earth with all of its mildew and mold, wearing my ugliest dress.

But as I came closer and closer to the Lord, I came to realize that death is only a door, both in the literal death of the body, and also in the death or crucifixion of the carnal flesh. And on the other side of that breaking of the clay pitcher, that earthen vessel, is the eternal light of God's joy.

The story of Gideon's army graphically demonstrates this breaking of the clay, whether the body in death or the crucifying of the carnal self. Gideon, God's mighty man of valor hiding behind the bushes, had a big army which became smaller and smaller as the Lord demanded commitment. When they were on the hillside so outnumbered and surrounded by the enemy, the Lord gave them a most unusual plan. He instructed them to take ordinary clay pitchers and put candles in them. Being desperate for any advice at all, they evidently figured, What have we got to lose?

And so the army, out-numbered outrageously by the enemy, hid their lights in clay pitchers and crept out into the darkness. In accordance with the Lord's plan, the people gave a great shout, the trumpets blew, and the pitchers were smashed, revealing instant light. The enemy was so frightened and so confused that they turned and killed one another. All that was left for Gideon's army to do was to gather the treasure.

And that's what God is doing with us. He is breaking the clay pitcher of our carnality so that God's light, the Light of Christ, can shine and the enemy will be confounded. Death is swallowed up in victory! The battle is His, and all that is left for us are the riches and honor of a life hidden in God.

BREAK: TO SEPARATE INTO PARTS

We can better understand this often-cataclysmic process of breaking when we study the definitions of the word Break and the applications to all levels of breaking both individually and corporately as the Body of Christ.

In this first definition we find the principle of separating or breaking into parts with suddenness or violence relating to that body of darkness that can be within us, or the body of pride, or the body of hurt. The sharp plow has broken apart that hard surface that has so bound itself together to resist the dealings of God. We must separate ourselves from that prison of darkness that often has such hold on our lives. To break indicates separation! The Word of God pierces to the dividing line of soul and spirit (Heb. 4:12).

Of course, that piercing, cutting, breaking process does contain an element of violence. Although it may seem harsh, discipline or correction, contrary to what is universally believed by so many, is not rejection. Discipline is simply an opportunity to obtain help in a progress of life that must go on with or without it. With God's loving correction, we move past our difficulties more quickly. Refusing discipline and correction simply prolongs and greatly complicates the job of the plow. The kingdom of God suffers violence, and violent men take it by force (Matt. 11:12). So be it. Let us apprehend the things of the Spirit. The breaking, the crucifixion of the flesh may not be gentle, pleasant, or fun. Through suffering, we enter the Kingdom. And the joyful resurrection life on the other side of suffering is for all eternity.

BREAKING OF THE CARNAL SELF. Jesus said, "Do not think that I came to bring peace on the earth; I did not come to bring peace, but a sword" (Matt. 10:34). That sword in operation in our lives, piercing to the dividing line of soul and spirit, will bring first a breaking in our perspective of self. The pride which resists so adamantly admissions that anything could NEED change or fixing is the first element of hardness which must be broken up and destroyed. Pride is the primary defender, exhorter, and promoter of self-life.

"Pride" is "an overly high opinion of one's self; exaggerated self-esteem, or conceit." What this would indicate in our lives is that our perspective has become so narrowed to self, that self becomes the only thing that we can see. It changes and colors our perspective, perception and discernment. This is an extremely dangerous place to be, since our vision becomes distorted and truth a slave to our own pride.

To humble ourselves under the mighty hand of God and allow the plow of the Lord to pierce and divide means that pride must be literally turned or plowed under. Humility could be said to be the opposite of pride, or the absence of pride or self-assertion. The word means "having or showing a consciousness of one's defects or shortcomings, not proud, not self-assertive, modest." It also means, "low in condition, rank, or position, lowly, unimportant, unpretentious." Jesus said,

> Come to Me, all you who labor and are heavy laden, and I will give you rest. Take My yoke upon you and learn from Me, for I am gentle and lowly in heart, and you will find rest for your souls. For My yoke is easy, and My burden is light. Matt. 11:28-30

So to be humble is to be lowly as Jesus was lowly. When we begin to contrast humility and pride, we find that we are contrasting self and the absence of self. Pride vs humility, and self vs the subjugation of self. Pride is stiff-necked. It doesn't want to bend; it doesn't want to turn its head to see other things or people, or the ideas of others. It doesn't want to be told what to do. But the absence of self is a broken and contrite heart, a teachable spirit desirous of being pleasing only to God.

Pride (or self) is pushy. Why can't I do that? I should have been the one. I'm not getting my "due." I am the best qualified. Pride pushes open its own doors, while humility says, You open the doors, Lord. Not my will but Thy will be done, Lord. Humility is like the Lamb of God who opened not His mouth, gentle and at rest.

Self is competitive, always comparing itself to others. I am much better at that. I can surpass them in excellence. I must be the best. I must excel no matter what. Humility displays a total lack of competition and a sincere desire and appreciation of the excellence in others. Humility (or the absence of self) is a teachable spirit which says, What can I learn from others? Teach me, Lord and show me the way in which I should go.

Although it prides itself in its own strength, self is actually weak. If I can't have it my way, I will quit. Humility is strong. Only Your will, Lord. In my weakness, Your strength is perfected. Self is resentful and quick to anger. The prideful spirit says, Don't step on my toes. Give me my right and my due. This situation is not fair. I deserved better than that. Humility is thankful, displaying a quiet spirit and surrendering all personal desire and ambition to the higher law of His grace.

The prideful selfish spirit is a stingy spirit. Is it worth my while? What's in it for me? The motives are impure because they are always related to how will it benefit me best? Humility is a generous, giving spirit that desires to lift up others and see that the glory only belongs to the Lord.

Self says, That's THEIR problem. Look at that huge log in their eye. But humility says, help me to love the one who hates me Lord. Help me to be more kind and patient, Lord. If I have offended, tell me how to make it right, Lord. Teach me your ways, O Lord.

Self is afraid to face its own limitations, thus carrying them to the grave. The humble spirit acknowledges, confesses and is healed of all limitations. The prideful self is so full of self that he can't see God. Humility puts self and God in the right order and thus begins to see God—and in seeing Him realizes his own finiteness. "Blessed are the pure in heart, for they shall see God" (Matt. 5:8).

The self that is bound only by its own confines has no hope. The humble and contrite spirit, the absence of pride, has hope eternal within. Plowing under the pride in our lives can only be a path of freedom and joy. The reward of humility and the fear of the Lord are riches, honor and life (Prov.22:4). Humility brings with it healing and forgiveness (2 Chron. 7:14), and ultimately, the humble and contrite heart will know triumph and exaltation (James 4:10). As we allow the plow of the Lord to break up the hardness of pride in our lives, to separate self from the humble heart, we liken ourselves to the humility of a child, the greatest in the kingdom of heaven (Matt. 18:4). Becoming as a child without guile, artifice or cunning will reveal another level in the character of our God.

The grace of our God, sufficient and without measure, is readily available to the humble (Prov.3:34). He who loses his life shall find it. In choosing what the prideful stiff-necked spirit would recognize as death, in choosing to lose that life, we will find the life of God.

> For thus says the high and exalted One Who lives forever, whose name is Holy, "I dwell on a high and holy place, and also with the contrite and lowly of spirit in order to revive the spirit of the lowly and to revive the heart of the contrite." Isa. 57:15

BREAK: TO END, CLOSE, OR DESTROY BY DISPERSING

When the plow attacks that hard crust across the face of a fallow field, it is ending, closing, or destroying the self-life. The plow closes open cracks, destroys harmful vegetation, and disperses debris. Then the field no longer simply exists, content in its selfish, lonely, fallow state, but is compelled by the plow to become fruitful and giving soil, allowing life to come forth for others.

We must come to the end of self. We must close the chapter of our will be done, If it feels good do it and To thine own self be true. In order that His kingdom come in our lives and His will be done in our lives as it is in Heaven, our will must end. Our will must be conformed, as His will becomes our own.

We destroy the carnal man of our lives by dispersing the darkness of self-life, of sensuality and idolatry, with the x-ray quality of God's light. Light always disperses darkness. We must come to the end and close the perspective given to us by the world. That perspective is a dry crack in the good soil, allowing the entrance of all kinds of deterrents to the growth of life. The plow will close those cracks and make way for HIS light to fill our eyes.

BREAK: TO BURST AND FORCE A WAY THROUGH

Breaking can also mean "to burst and force a way through; to make or effect by cutting, forcing, or pressing through." Here again we see that sense of force, violence, and power. To submit to the power of God must always be the easier course than to stiffen the neck and resist that same force. We can, by an act of our will, cut the chains that bind and allow the plow of God to boldly come through our earth. It is a choice. "But I press on in order that I may lay hold of that for which also I was laid hold of by Christ Jesus" (Phil. 3:12).

Cutting and pressing through the flesh is literally making our way into His Presence. Just as the veil in the temple was rent and Jesus' flesh was torn and broken, so the veil of our flesh must be rent that we may see and display His eternal glory. The kingdom of God is within us—Christ in us the hope of glory. The living waters within us, out of our belly, burst forth with the resurrection life of God. Snipping and cutting away the veil of flesh releases more and more of a free flow of the life of God, healing and illuminating not only ourselves but those around us.

BREAK: TO ESCAPE BY FORCE FROM JAIL

Another definition of "to break," is "to make ineffective as a binding force, to escape by force from jail." One of the saddest things about addiction and idolatry is that often the victim is not aware that it is a binding force. Often that thing which seems the most comfortable to us is actually binding us and keeping us imprisoned. Once I was ministering in a certain city. A group of people had gathered and were sharing their problems. A man began to confess his addiction to food. What struck me most was that over and over he kept saying that food addiction was so much worse than addiction to alcohol. It had not occurred to the man that it was a spirit that he was fighting, in either case.

So many people don't even recognize that they are being driven and affected by spirits. How effective that weapon is when it is not recognized as a weapon of the enemy. When we are imprisoned in spirit, we are in just as much bondage as if we are in a physical jail. But whom the Son sets free is free indeed! Sometimes the effecting of that freedom is not without pain. Often we expect a lightning bolt from heaven to come and completely change us. But unfortunately, in many cases that power can be unleashed only by repentance.

Jonah was a prophet under orders. But being a rebellious and disobedient prophet, he got on a ship going in a different direction than God had told him to go. A storm arose, and even the heathen on the ship recognized that the storm was a judgment. Someone was at fault. When they cast lots to uncover the culprit, the lot fell upon Jonah. It wasn't until Jonah left the vehicle of his disobedience, that the people were saved and the storm was quieted. When he said yes to the Lord, then he was free and on his way to accomplish God's errand. But the freedom of others depended upon Jonah's freedom. How often in the Body of Christ is that the case? The freedom of others depends on our freedom, and our freedom depends on repentance and breaking—separation of death from life in our lives.

BREAK: TO DISRUPT THE ORDER OF

"To break" also means "to disrupt the order or compactness of; to invalidate a will by legal action." There are two plans for our lives. Of course, the Lord of Glory, Who knew our form long before it was knit in our mother's womb, has a divine purpose for each of us who were bought with a price and covered with His grace. But satan has another plan, carefully constructed and being carried out with diabolical cleverness. "You are of your father the devil, and you want to do the desires of your father" (John 8:44) When we become born-again, we disrupt the comfortable plans of the enemy. But he does regroup. We must continue to disrupt those plans by seeking constantly the will and plan of GOD the Father, and, in obedience, following that plan. Our covenant, our "will" is made with our Heavenly Father, and submitting to the sharp two-edged sword cuts and severs over and over again the counterfeit agreements drawn up by our enemy.

A popular song several years ago was sung by a new Christian, "You've Got to Serve Somebody." We all will serve one or the other, day by day, hour by hour. By holding on to greed, lust, apathy, and many other sins, we are willfully following and serving SOMEONE'S plan. Whose is it?? It is the will of God that we inherit His promises and take our rightful legal authority over death in our lives, over satan, and over our flesh. When we do this we invalidate the inheritance satan intends for us: death and destruction and everlasting torment. We have the authority and it involves BREAKING.

BREAK: TO DEFEAT UTTERLY DESTROY

The last definition of "break" that we will investigate is "to defeat utterly and end as an effective force—destroy; to crush the spirit of." The ultimate purpose of Jesus' appearing is clearly stated in 1 John 3:7-8. Little children, let no one deceive you; the one who practices righteousness is righteous, just as He is righteous; the one who practices sin is of the devil; for the devil has sinned from the beginning. The Son of God appeared for this purpose, that He might destroy the works of the devil.

And He says again in John 10:10b, "I am come that ye might have life and life more abundantly." The purpose of the evil one is contrasted in the verse before (John 10:10a), "The thief comes only to steal, and kill, and destroy." Jesus has placed in our hands the power to choose that which would be destroyed in our lives: the light and life of God and our hope, or the darkness and temptations of satan. The battle is ultimately spirit: we break by the power of the sword of the Spirit (the blade of the plow), the spirit of death, the spirits of darkness and the pride and lust of the flesh.

> But may it never be that I should boast except in the cross of our Lord Jesus Christ, through which the world has been crucified to me, and I to the world. Gal. 6:14

> Now those who belong to Christ Jesus have crucified the flesh with its passions and desires. Gal. 5:24

THE TRIUMPH OF BREAKING

Many of us have heard so many sermons about death to self and death to the enemy that hearing even the title of another often makes us groan. We have been taught the message of crucifixion without the triumph of the resurrection which must follow. There is a TRIUMPH in the breaking of the earth! There is a TIME for it! "A time to kill, and a time to heal; A time to break down, and a time to build up" (Eccl. 3:3).

By the plow, we not only break down, cut asunder and turn over, we break INTO a new day! "Until the day break, and the shadows flee away turn, my beloved; and be thou like a roe, or a young hart, upon the mountains of Bether" (S.S. 2:17, KJV). The breaking of earth in our lives signals the day breaking and the coming of our beloved. "Then your light will break out like the dawn, and your recovery will speedily spring forth; and your righteousness will go before you; the glory of the Lord will be your rear guard" (Isa.58:9). The Hebrew word for "break" here is "baqa", "to rend, break, rip, or open." "Break forth into singing" (Isa.44:23). We are breaking out of death into life, joy and singing.

Once I was praying with a friend of mind and she had a vision. She said that the vision was for me, and began to describe what she was seeing. She saw a flat field stretching as far as the eye could see, the ground covered everywhere with hundreds of pieces of broken clay pottery. The voice of the Lord began to speak and He said, "I have been breaking and breaking and breaking and breaking. . ." As His voice continued to speak "and breaking," a great light began to shine on the broken pieces. Instantly they were transformed into colorful bits of stained glass that were transparent with light.

Then as she watched, the Lord spoke, "Now watch what I will do, now watch what I will do, now watch what I will do." As His voice continued, all of the pieces were swept up into a magnificent vase, effervescent with light. Suddenly, out of the vase began to shoot fountains of water, catching the light and flashing rainbows abroad. And the Lord was continuing to say, "Now watch what I will do, now watch what I will do." The water was cascading over the sides and flowing down when she saw at the base of the vase hundreds and thousands of people. As the water reached the people, they began to be swept away with the power and force of the living water.

The breaking of the vessel transformed it by God's beauty and power into a life-giving vessel sweeping many into the river whose streams make glad the city of God.

At the time of her vision I was working my way out of several great traumas in my life, and depression and heaviness were continuing to hold back my joy as I still could not see ahead the triumphant work of the Lord's destiny in my broken life. Her vision was a tremendous encouragement to me of God's power and overcoming grace on my behalf.

The Lord has been hard at work tilling and cultivating the earth, plowing and turning over, and breaking the soil of His garden. Throughout ages past, He has tilled and cultivated. Now in this season He is saying through the mouths of His prophets with a great triumphant shout, "Now watch what I will do! Now watch what I will do!" The greatest flood of living water that the world has ever seen is on the brink of the horizon, about to pour through the broken clay vessels of His Body made brilliant in His Light.

In another powerful act of Jesus, the incarnate Word, He broke the bread offering of a small boy and fed a multitude. The disciples couldn't understand that He would break the Bread of His Life and feed the nations for all time.

> And it came about that when He had reclined at the table with them, He took the bread and blessed it, and breaking it, He began giving it to them. And their eyes were opened and they recognized Him; and He vanished from their sight. Luke 24:30-31

Now many of us cry, "I must have more of God, I must know more of Him." We cannot seem to detach ourselves from the concept that God is somewhere far away and He is going to "come" and visit us so that we can know Him better. And Almighty God is saying, "I am inside of you. You have only to open your eyes in the breaking of the bread and recognize Me." The Lord has opened my eyes to see that there is so much of God released in my voice, in teaching, in prophetic words, in my daily life that I have not seen, because I haven't recognized God's Spirit in it. More and more He is bringing us all to the place where we can recognize Him. Our eyes must be opened so that we can recognize Who and What is God and who and what is not God. We must recognize the precious and powerful treasure of the Kingdom living inside us.

It was not until Jesus broke the bread that the eyes of those who loved Him were opened and they recognized Him. As we are broken like bread to feed the hungry, the eyes of the nations will be opened, and they will see

59

Jesus. He can only shine through broken vessels. The breaking, and plowing of the soil of our lives allows the divine Seed to burst forth and shine with the blinding Light and Glory of Restored Creation. The triumph of the fruitful Garden is the inheritance and joy of the heart of a loving Plowman.

IV

Plowmen Of God

The plowman ought to plow in hope, and the thresher ought to
thresh in expectation of partaking of the harvest.
1 Corinthians 9:10b AMP

*Central thought: The plowman rose early while even the birds were still
asleep, and he worked until the light was gone. He lived close to the earth.
He was in touch with it. He was in touch with the feel and the smell and the
sight and the sound of the earth. And as the plow pushed through the dirt,
and the arduous labor trained muscles upon muscles, he would glory in the
sun upon his back and the wind upon his face, in the songs of the birds and
most of all, he would joy in the sight of the rows upon rows of freshly turned
earth about to receive the seed, the seed of life, seed that would multiply
and become food to feed the nations.*

THE PLOWMAN

As we explore the principles of plowing and planting, with all of the
underlying types and shadows, we realize that the plowmen (the sowers, the
husbandmen) working hand in hand with the Lord of the Harvest must be
most unique and diversified individuals. The plowmen of God march on
inner orders and to the beat of different drums than those in the mainstream
of life concerned with tent-making alone. God nurtures and develops the
hearts of all those called according to His purpose, carefully sharpening,
shaping and polishing these most precious gems who will care for, feed,

and equip the Body of Christ and the world for the furtherance of the Kingdom.

God causes the growth, His is the grace, and His the life-force and direction of all experiences of labor in the fields and vineyards of the King. The husbandmen of the Lord of the Harvest encounter many unique situations and obstacles which develop character and great flexibility. They learn to be instant in and out of season (2 Tim. 4:2). They learn to live one day at a time, with a clear understanding of the finished work. They learn to depend on God.

As we meditate upon these unique and stalwart servants of the Most High, let us explore some of their characteristics and the situations surrounding this challenging work.

> I planted, Apollos watered, but God was causing the growth. So then neither the one who plants nor the one who waters is anything, but God who causes the growth. Now he who plants and he who waters are one; but each will receive his own reward according to his own labor. For we are God's fellow workers; you are God's field, God's building. 1 Cor. 3:6-10

LOVE FOR THE EARTH

In the hearts of God's plowmen dwells an abiding love of the earth: the sight, smell, sound and feel of the earth. Wherever they go, the earth cries out, calling and pulling on them, because these little bits of earth see in them the heart of the husbandman, the heart of the tiller of the soil who likes to clean them up. Plowmen have a heart that loves to work with people, which requires getting past the surface to see them as God sees them. The plowman's heart can see past the hardness, the weeds and thorns, the unlovely and uncomely, and into the nature and texture of soil that can be trained and tilled to shelter the Seed of God.

A plowman, a farmer in the business of tilling the soil, loves the earth, as he must lest he become a bitter and discouraged farmer. If he hates what he is doing, he will not be good at it. Consequently, people who are true farmers wouldn't choose to do anything else. Most of the time people look at them and think, "I wouldn't do what they are doing for anything on the face of the earth!" But the tiller of the soil has a zeal for the earth that others find difficult to understand.

"The love of God is greater far than tongue or pen can ever tell," so the old song goes. All the giftings, talents and education in the universe are but sounding gongs and clanging cymbals without love. Faithfulness to duty, earnestness, diligence, all the fervor possible in a man of flesh, will only produce houses built on sand—without love. First and foremost in the Father's heart and purpose is love.

> Behold what manner of love the Father has bestowed on us, that
> we should be called children of God. 1 John 3:1a NKJV

Love is selfless in nature, focused on the welfare and well-being of the beloved. God is developing in His plowmen an all-encompassing love for the earthen vessels housing His seed. "For the love of Christ compels us (1 Cor. 5:14a, NKJ). The heart of the Father is invading His army and transforming His plowmen, His sowers, and His reapers into soldiers of love. "By this all men will know that you are My disciples, if you have love for one another" (John 13:35).

BREAD OF MISUNDERSTANDING

Many who operate by love have eaten much of the bread of misunderstanding. Separated from their more worldly peers by the river of God, they are often criticized for motives, actions, and personal characteristics. These ministers are plowmen who are often disrespected even though they accomplish large quantities of hot, dirty, backbreaking work, the greater part of which is unseen.

I have a friend in another country who calls me about every three months. We usually talk for an hour, or an hour and a half on the phone. She loves to hear all that I do. Then each time I tell her all that I do, she says, "I just get exhausted! I call you every three months to hear what you are doing and it wears me out just hearing about it on the telephone!" I think she calls to encourage herself because she knows the large amount of work that she does herself. When she calls me and finds out what I do, it makes her feel better. She tells me that when she hangs up she has much more energy than she had when she called. She takes joy in hearing stories about the work of the plowman.

But there are many others who do not have the vision of what lies beyond the work. The plowman knows that the season of plowing will one day be over and the time will come when the seed drops into the earth. Then the green shoots come up, and the time of harvesting the grain will come. There will be the baking of the bread, and people will be fed. The plowman sees the end from the beginning and plans his work accordingly.

But too many people see the work and not the fruit. Others realize and are excited by the fruit, but have no idea of the amount of work and sacrifice involved. When people around us do not understand the vision to which we are called, we have a perfect opportunity to practice the patience and grace of the Lord. They do not understand the cycles of life-giving and continuing growth.

PLOW DIVERSIFIED FIELDS

One year early in my ministry, I was ministering in several different capacities at once. I was the minister of music at a local church. I had been speaking at various meetings, and in the midst of it all, I began to make banners. Banner-making was a new and challenging ministry. The Lord had plans to use me as a pioneer in a controversial and unknown area.

First, I had to pioneer in my own home. I was spending all of my spare time at home in my dining room with sequins and materials everywhere, making banners; but my husband was paying for them. For the first two or three years he paid for everything. He had no idea what this crazy woman was doing with these banners or the spiritual significance of it. I didn't fully know it myself, and it would be years before anyone could accept that it had anything to do with revealing spiritual truth. The faithfulness of a husband who not only tolerated what I was doing but also financed it is a special gift from God. He didn't always do it with a joyful heart, because he was not the one with the vision. But God says blessed are they who have seen but more blessed are they who have not seen and yet believed (John 20:29).

We must understand that people who seem to be fighting against us because they don't understand a vision will be even more blessed once they finally believe. One day some will be able to embrace the spirit that says, "I may not understand what you are doing, but I bless you in the name of Jesus."

Each one of us who are plowmen must have that same attitude toward all of our fellow workers who are plowing different fields. They may not plow exactly the way we plow. They may not use the same kind of equipment that we use. They may have a different set of circumstances as far as droughts and storms and different kinds of soil. Soil is very complex. Certainly, the heart of man is complex. God is going to use plowmen with diverse instruments and distinctive ways of approaching these things, however all are necessary in diversity of fields and vision.

TOLERANCE NEEDED

It is so important that we develop tolerance for one another and for other ministers, other plowmen in other fields. Once there was a certain minister who taught at a large conference I attended. If I decided to analyze with my natural mind what he taught, I would disagree with everything that he said. Basically, it was a prosperity message, a how-to-wring-money-out-of-everybody message. Everything taught in the Word of God was used toward that end. Formulas on making money were extracted from passages of scripture and expounded upon. I am simply not called to plow that particular field. So I could have had ambivalent feelings about the way this person ministered.

I was instructed to remember not to touch God's anointed, and not to lean upon my own understanding. What I sow I will reap and to the measure I mete it out, it will be measured back to me. What another minister does and how he does it is between him and God. He may be plowing a very necessary field for reasons that I have no ability to comprehend. If he has revelation in an area that I do not, then I am in the precarious position of criticizing something of which I have no knowledge. I have already stopped the flow of the Spirit in my own life which might enlighten me in a new area. Then by my unteachable attitude inspired by strong opinion, I have stopped learning.

Suppose that in the natural realm, you are an extremely opinionated person. You are physically a meticulously manicured person who is never smudged or dirty, and one hair is never out of place. In passing one day, you see your neighbor out in his field plowing. He has dirt under his fingernails, he is sweaty, he smells, and you are on your way to the grocery store to buy bread. You are criticizing him for his occupation. You are disgusted with his physical person, disdainful and haughty, placing him beneath and yourself above. What you don't realize is that he is working to put the bread in the store that you're on your way to buy with your pristine pure hands.

We can see that principle at work in the Body of Christ. What affects the toe affects the finger, and what affects the ear affects the nose. What is done to and for one part of the Body affects all. We are all a part of the same Body and those who are criticized and ostracized may very well be putting the bread on the table that we are about to eat!

The networking of the Holy Spirit is truly amazing! Invariably as we travel around the world, we will meet someone in Malaysia, who is a close friend of the person in the U.S. that we just saw last week. The Lord causes the world to seem so small and links His people together in such infinite and intricate ways. We will arrive to minister in a conference and find out that it has all been put together with people from various places where we have ministered. Then when everyone comes together, we quickly realize the enormous intertwining of God's people across the world.

INVOLVED IN DIRTY WORK

So a plowman is one who digs, and in digging, he gets stained with the very earth in which he works. In the spiritual realm, we often walk unsuspectingly in unclean places and find ourselves needing the cleansing of the water of the Word. Once I was involved in a truly phenomenal conference over one weekend. All over the world we have never seen the Lord top the amazing corporate work done in this particular people. Immediately after the benediction, God began to move.

Just as our ministry team was rejoicing at what God had done, a terrible confrontation happened between two of the main leaders of the participating congregations. The fact that something like that could come about after what had just happened in God was so frustrating. We got back to the hotel and sat on the side of the bed and stared, fighting frustration and rage.

Dirt under the fingernails of the plowman can come as a shock. He has, before his very eyes, seen the plowman overtake the reaper; he has plowed, planted, and seen the seeds not only grow up but be harvested and the bread baked all in one weekend. Then the un-regenerated earth rears up and rejects the work of the Lord by manifesting its old dead nature. The frustration brought to the laborer by working with resistant soil is part of the labor.

Many times after we have been ministering, ascending to the heights in the Lord and seeing Him do such wonderful things, we go home and get into immediate strife with our family. Mud that needs to be washed off can get on everybody. I once heard a famous evangelist say that he can conduct a prayer line and go home to the hotel room and have to spend two hours in the Word washing himself off because he is so dirty. As workers of the soil, we cannot allow that aspect of our labor to bond with us or to cause hatred of the earth. There must simply be a continual washing of the water of the Word. Many hours can be spent preparing for a service, then teaching, preaching, praying and prophesying. Instead of assuming that we have been laboring with the Lord and now need to "relax," we may consider refreshing ourselves anew in the Presence of the Lord and His Word.

WORK AND PLAY

The plowman is a person that really doesn't have much extra time for what he once called "fun." Those of you who have gone into full-time ministry suddenly realize that you don't do many things just for "fun" anymore. The principal is that you learn to enjoy what you are doing. You learn not to call it work because the work is the Lord's. You learn that in the midst of the "work" is where life is. It is no longer you who live, but Christ Who lives within you.

Soon all that once was relaxation falls away before the exhilaration of the moving of God's Spirit. Excitement at the miracles of God, the transforming nature of His power, and the inexpressible joy of His laughter, quickly and easily transcends any momentary pleasure that the world can give. When going into any kind of ministry you learn not to compare it to a natural job.

One day I was riding in a car with my husband and some friends of ours who work at a famous government agency. They were talking about salaries, grumbling and complaining about how the cost of living goes up x percent but their salary raise isn't x percent, in effect complaining that they are actually losing money as they go. I opened my mouth and out came, "I can't imagine getting paid for what you do." Silence filled the car. The next week our friend sent my ministry a check! New perspective had hit him. I work eight hours a day, but I get paid for it. This is someone who goes and spends three months on the other side of the world working all hours of the day and night and paid their own way to go! All of a sudden it put things in perspective. We can't count the cost. All that does is open the door for resentment and bitterness and a spirit that feels unappreciated, unrecognized, and unremunerated. There is no price on eternal seed, eternal growth or eternal gain. We simply open the door to God's joy and His Presence becomes the only "reward" or fun needed.

SINGLE-MINDED

The plowman has no time to count the hours. His whole concentration, his whole focus, the only thing that he notices is the earth he has been sent to till. That is where his gaze falls and where his heart is. He is single minded. Like dove's eyes, the plowman's eyes are single, seeing only the earth that he loves and the transformation in progress.

As a plowman in ministry, you will not dwell on how your back hurts, or how tired you are, or how much longer will this last. You will look only at the heart of the soil and not on the cost or the toll taken. Just think if Jesus had counted the cost. What He saw with His natural eyes were people that He had raised up denying that they even knew Him. He was a God-Man Who did not judge by the seeing of His eye or the hearing of His ear. Jesus knew His mission and the cost, and went forth doing the will of His Father.

The plowman looks straight into the heart, like God! We must see no man except in Christ (1 Cor. 5:16). That means that instead of seeing Jane, I see the Christ in Jane. I see the condition of her soil that she has allowed to be molded and tilled. I see the fruit manifesting everywhere in her life. I see all of the things that Christ is in her. I don't look at her and wish her personality were different or that she had a better vocabulary. Jane's Husbandman is the lover of her soul, and he perfects those things which concern her.

Singleness of eye enables the plowman to remain unmoved and unruffled by the distractions and impediments aimed at hindering his work and dampening his spirits. Even as his eye remains focused on the seed rather than the dirt, so also is it stayed on the Father of Life, Who fills all in all with His mighty power.

A SHARP EYE AND A SHARP INSTRUMENT

To look into the heart, to make a place for the seed in the midst of unlovely soil, demands a sharpness of eye and a keen sense of discernment. Many of us in the Body of Christ are like a camera that stays a little out of focus. When we prophesy, move in the Spirit or teach, it is not always clear or easily understood. When we pray, it may seem indistinct. As plowmen we refocus the camera lens and sharpen the sight so that when we shoot, we shoot to the heart of the matter. The Lord is excising all of the extraneous material and the blurred edges so that we can shoot straight and true in cooperating with the living Word. We always remember that these are matters of the Spirit, and our understanding must be by the spirit and not our natural, carnal mind. His view is always sharp!

Depending solely upon exceptional education and superior training is transformed as the Lord readies leaders who learn to depend on the Lord and His wisdom, might and power. He is taking us out of our comfort zones and forcing us to do things in which our only course is to depend upon Him. We are plowmen who do a little of everything so that our dependence in every instance is on Him. "To the weak I became weak, that I might win the weak; I have become all things to all men, that I may by all means save some" (1 Cor. 9:22). This surely sharpens our focus and discernment out of sheer desperation!

The blade used to cut into the earth must be kept whetted and sharpened to both minimize the energy expenditure and maximize the quality of the job done. As a workman who needs not to be ashamed, God's plowmen are learning to be firmly grounded in the Word, His wisdom and power, that His moving through us be sharp, swift and clear.

The sharpness of eye renders the plowman equipped with the gift of discernment—the ability to see with the all-wise and knowing gaze of the Father. As we earnestly desire spiritual gifts (1 Cor. 14:1), our loving Father extends to us all that is necessary for the task accorded us. The plowman will use his keen eye for skillful tilling, pruning, and weeding. As we exercise words of wisdom and knowledge, the gift of discernment of spirits combines to cleanse the earth before us on its way to malleable soil and healthy crops.

STAMINA IN BATTLE

One of the primary character traits that we must have as plowmen is stamina. Glory to God! A plowman is one who battles the elements on behalf of the soil, on behalf of the seed, on behalf of the life that he has been given to wrest out of an unrepentant, hard, and rebellious earth. He battles on behalf of the seed. In the midst of the battle we must remember, "I'm battling on behalf of the seed in Susan, on behalf of the seed in John, on behalf of the seed of life inside God's people." Regardless of how the earth responds or how it doesn't respond, the plowman must remain single-minded, loving the earth, steadfast and with such stamina that he is immovable.

Stamina. Here I will try to describe to you one day on the mission field several years ago. This was truly a day to focus and keep moving while remaining immovable in purpose no matter what. It was about ninety percent humidity and one hundred degrees Fahrenheit. There was no air-conditioning, and no ice or cool drink. Cars were tin boxes designed to hold in as much heat as possible. After about five weeks in cultures different from my experience, I hadn't had anything to eat that I recognized in so long that I was actually getting thin (good news, but only up to a point).

We arrived in a large city where the electricity goes off every day but you never know when. We were staying in a beautiful home with lovely friends in the ministry. Have you ever seen lather on a horse? That's what we all looked like all the time. We won't discuss the smell. We rode across the hot, crowded city with extreme pollution problems to preach at an afternoon meeting. Immediately after we started the meeting, the electricity went off. We ministered the entire afternoon meeting in the dark in extreme heat. We rode back to the house in one of the metal boxes on wheels that had heated up to at least one hundred and fifty degrees. The traffic was terrible. We rode for an hour and a half in bumper to bumper traffic, breathing fumes.

When we got back to the house and walked in the door, we had less than an hour to get ready to leave for a huge revival meeting (they were expecting thirty thousand people) on the other side of the city. We're not even discussing food. Food hadn't been thought of in so long. (Remember there's no ice.) The electricity was also off at the house. There never was hot water at the house, but with the electricity off there was not one drop of any kind of water. We're talking NO WATER. None to brush your teeth with. Horse sweat, you name it, it didn't matter how we smelled. There was NO WATER. With no electricity, there was no air conditioning. If there had just been water, I could have wet myself down and at least created a draft. So we wiped the sweat off and sprayed perfume on and went back through the bumper to bumper traffic in the hot van to the other side of town to the meeting.

At the meeting, we had been invited to minister in prophetic song and dance just before the last half of the service. They had requested that I be dressed in my dance garments and on stage during praise and worship. The air conditioning was also off at the revival arena. They were using the generators to run lights. Thirty thousand people had gathered in this one building with no windows.

The person entrusted with my costume had disappeared. I didn't know if she had my garments, wherever she was. I had fifteen minutes to put on the many layers of clothing demanded by modesty and I couldn't find my costume. So I ran back and forth backstage, up and down, running everywhere looking for my garments. I finally located them, as the minutes ticked away, outside in the parking lot in a LOCKED VAN.

Then I began the marathon to find the keys. At last I found the person, found the keys, retrieved the garments, and made it panting to the dressing room which proved to be a windowless room of intense and over-powering heat. I got everything on with great difficulty, pulling it on over all that sweat and rushed out onto the stage in my many layers of clothing topped with heavy sequins. I stood there dressed for the arctic, and we had bank after bank of lights, all trained on the stage like heat lamps.

We were not introduced. Nobody knew who we were or what we were doing and after the last song, I walked from one side of the stage to the other, sat down at an electric instrument that I had never seen in my life before with thirty-six keys instead of eighty-eight and started playing a prophetic song while my minister friend sang. I was so hot that sweat was dripping off my face onto the keys. I had a woman dotting my face like a surgeon at the operating table so that I could keep my hands on the keys. The people had no idea what we were doing. Some thought we were performing a carefully rehearsed opera. Then as soon as we finished the spontaneous prophetic song, I got up from the instrument and walked to the center of the stage and danced. This was focusing on the Lord in the midst of the storm.

In a situation like this you cannot be moved by emotion or physical discomfort. There were thirty thousand people stacked into the building, live television, and eight thousand people outside watching on video who couldn't get in. They were all hungry for God and desperate for His presence, many unsaved, needing to be introduced to the Redeemer. Even in physically trying circumstances we must operate in the Spirit, allowing His power to move to touch, heal and deliver.

His strength and His stamina sustain us in the most rigorous battle!

We are still hearing stories of the miraculous things that God did by His Spirit in that challenging series of meetings in a revival arena hotter with the fire of God than with the natural heat. The Lord is growing us into plowmen who are unmoved by drought, unmoved by storms, unmoved by famine, unmoved that we must plow up a field so full of rocks that just hauling them away would take a hundred men. We will be unmoved and we will believe the Word when it says, Nothing is impossible with God! Nothing! I can do all things through Christ Who strengthens me.

AGGRESSIVE

The plowman must exhibit aggressive behavior in the task that is set before him. This is not a job for lightweights, physical or spiritual. The days of sitting back and waiting for lightning to strike are over. The faucet of Living Water is inside of us and every day we have the ability to turn the faucet on or off. It is a river that must never be dammed up or hindered in any way. We are to be aggressive in releasing the rivers of God. The Kingdom of God suffers violence and the violent take it by force (Matt.11:12). The plowman has to be aggressive. The only way to plow a straight furrow is to put the hand to the plow and move forward with determination. He will literally wrest the life out of that earth.

Many times ministers are criticized because of the manner in which they minister personally to people in services. Before I became one, I was so skeptical about any display of emotion, any evidence of power (I thought of it more as force at the time). Anything that looked aggressive on the part of the minister, I immediately classified as forceful flesh. But as I began to experience the power and anointing of the Holy Spirit to transform His people myself, I had to readjust my attitudes.

Knowing about all the incidences in the Word where human beings fell to the ground at the Presence of the Lord, it still came as a distinct shock when I saw people I was hardly touching fall under the power of God. Many times, I found that in order to keep my hands in contact with them I had to follow them as they went back (these are the ones who went more slowly, some dropped like rocks). It was amusing to realize that from the spectator's point of view, it probably looked the opposite of what was really happening:

that they were going because I was pushing, instead of the truth that I was following because they were going first! I had to rethink and repent for all those ministers I had criticized in the past!

Once while ministering in Toronto, I was taken on a side trip to Niagara Falls. As I stood and gazed at the absolutely violent outpouring of thundering water, I cried out to the Living God. Let the flow of Your Spirit thunder through me with just that unending, unmeasured, aggressive flow! When the spirit and power of Elijah is unleashed freely out of this end-time generation, opinions and judgments of man will take a back seat to the accomplishing of the purposes of God and we will see an unmeasured harvest of His miracle-working power.

DISAPPOINTMENT IN EARTH

The plowman often feels that he is fighting a losing battle with time. Have you every ministered to someone over and over and finally they die? Some you pray for get even more violently ill right after you pray. Since you feel you are fighting a losing battle, discouragement becomes a familiar companion. Imagine the plowmen back in the 1700's when they first came to a new country and the plow had to do its work and the seed had to grow just so and the seasons had to be in proper order just for civilization to stay alive. Imagine how discouraged they were when a drought came or the locusts ate up the crop. But God does not get discouraged. I'm sure that when Adam fell God did not wring His hands and cry nervous tears. Viewing God's work from God's perspective is a vital must at all times.

We ministered several times at an inner-city church in a large southern city. It was a new and exciting challenge every time we went. Witches and warlocks often passed up and down on the streets outside the church (visible to the entire congregation through the storefront windows which opened directly onto the sidewalk) and hurled curses at us as we were preaching. As leaders, we went out at midnight many nights after the evening service to topless bars on the strip to witness to the people on the streets. The witches followed us hurling curses and we pressed on, hurling back Words of Life.

The entire church was made up of people who had been saved off the streets and out of the bars, and it was a remarkable time. In this place, we plowmen saw incredible fruit. To the degree that they were wild without the Lord, they became wild for the Lord. Miraculous things were happening. The church was multiplying. Then we lost contact with the pastor for a time. We found out later that he and his wife were separated, the church had completely disbanded, and the sheep were scattered, wounded and confused.

In a situation like that, what do you say? This is a place where we, as well as many others, labored hard, long hours. And we saw fruit. Each time we went back, we saw more and more fruit. Yet all of a sudden, it looked as though the fruit was stolen and the fields despoiled. But even though the existing structure in the natural seems destroyed, God looks upon the heart. He is the husbandman of the field. This side of Glory, we may never know the extent of the work done in the individual hearts that gave them the ability to survive in victory in spite of the onslaughts of the enemy. We continue to judge not by the seeing of the eye or decide by the hearing of the ear (Isa. 11:3).

A friend of mine who had been having a lot of trouble was telling me one night, "I've been cursing God. Am I going to go to hell because I curse God, because I yell at God?" She was overwhelmed by fear, guilt, and condemnation. So I said, "Do you know what your yelling at God is like?" And she said, "What?" And I said, "About like an ant cursing an elephant. I don't think that ant is going to make the elephant very nervous."

I certainly am not condoning cursing God, we must keep the onslaughts of the enemy in perspective and remember that God is great. His mighty and awesome power is not hampered and hindered by the minuscule machinations of man. We cannot stop the purposes of God, and we cannot judge them by our standards. They may become rearranged from the pattern we thought they would take, but He will prevail, and He will accomplish that which He sets forth concerning His own.

UNEXPECTED FRUIT

It is always a delight—and just like God—to be surprised when you least expect it with evidence of His wondrous power, often combined with a unique and captivating sense of humor. I got home late one night from a ministry trip, absolutely exhausted. I discovered that I had a doctor's appointment early the next morning. When I remembered that I had scheduled it, I was not pleased. I decided that I was going to get up at nine o'clock and call and cancel it. So I got up at nine o'clock and the Lord said, "No, I want you to go."

My doctor is a Christian, full of the Spirit of God. I went in to my appointment and sat down. When he came in for the pre-exam talk, I began discussing with him my upcoming trip around the world, in order to get medicines and other things that I might need for such a long trip to remote locations. I could tell that the more I talked about it, the more upset he got.

Finally, he erupted and said, "I've just got to talk to somebody! Here I am and I chat with God and I say, 'Here I am. Do you see me? Here I am! I'm waiting and why isn't it happening yet?' Then somebody like you comes in and tells me you're going all over the world. And I say to Him, 'Listen, she's going all over the world! Why is it her and not me?'" (Keep in mind this is my doctor speaking.) He stopped in midstream and said, "I don't know why I'm telling you all this! I normally don't tell all my problems to my patients." I said, "Well, it could be because I am a minister." That was all he needed. The dam had burst and his heart was opened.

I could already hear his nurse going to all of his other rooms and telling everyone, "He will be right with you. Don't think that we have forgotten about you." So he had all these people waiting in all these rooms and he is down in my room getting spiritual counsel. I said, "Listen, could I say a prayer with you?" He said, "Sure." He laid down his notebook and all his stuff. I took his hand and prayed for him and gave him the Word of the Lord. He said, "I'm so glad you came by today. I feel so much better." I said, "Praise God!"

The Plowmen of the Lord must be ready to plow at any moment. This opens the door to be blessed by the unexpected moving of the Lord in fields we don't normally work. What a joy to be the instrument of the Lord in the eternal fields of the Kingdom!

REMEMBER WONDROUS WORKS OF LIFE

The plowman or husbandman of the Lord isn't always in a state of encouragement! When the fields or conditions are difficult, we focus on the amazing works the Lord has already done. David the psalmist in the midst of discouragement said, "O my God, my soul is in despair within me; therefore I remember Thee from the land of the Jordan, and the peaks of Hermon, from Mount Mizar" (Psa. 42:6). In troubled times, he remembered and enumerated the wondrous works of the Lord. The wonderful memories of all the things He has done are like candles of light shining in the darkness. The more these memories are gathered together, the brighter the darkness will become. Plowmen must encourage themselves in the Lord. When David's son was sick, he fasted in sackcloth and ashes, but when the boy died, David got up and washed himself, changed his clothes and encouraged himself in the Lord.

An example that I always remember in these times never fails to delight my soul, even today. Once we ministered in a conference held in a church that seemed to be dying. Though the building and grounds were spectacular, the people had dwindled to a handful of faithfuls who were starving for revival. So we went in with a team of about fifty incredible folks. We had as many people as they did.

We started on Friday night. The pastor had advertised it and there were several other churches in town there. When we started the Friday night service, it was like death. The people were subdued and unresponsive. The only people in the whole church responding in worship were our team. There seemed to be a strong binding spirit which held the people in an almost skeptical state of unbelief. We sang. We danced. We prophesied. The Word of the Lord was taught through drama. Then I preached on releasing the living waters out of the midst of Mount Zion. When we love the Lord our God with all of our heart (spirit), all of our mind (soul) and all of our strength (body), we will worship Him in manifested expressions of all three. Worshipping Him in Spirit and in Truth demands that all three parts of our being respond to His Presence in scriptural ways: shouting, singing, dancing, kneeling, standing, and bowing.

As I taught and then led the people in doing what they had learned, I watched grave clothes flying off. By the end of the Friday night service, they were free of self-consciousness, free of doubt and inhibition, free to worship Him in extravagant love and Truth. We went into a powerful prophetic flow which continued for the rest of the weekend as my minister friends and I continued to teach on the prophetic and powerful Voice of the Lord.

On Sunday morning we had a communion service. As we prophesied and ministered to the people, a group of teenage girls who happened to be passing by the church heard the music and came in. I didn't know that they weren't members of the church. A woman brought one of them to me, saying, "these girls are scared to death." One girl looked to be about 14 years old with wild blond hair, wearing a black leather jacket and smelling of cigarette smoke. She was lost, steeped in rebellious "freedom" and miserable. The girl got saved, filled with the Spirit, and was hugging me and crying. In just an instant, a precious life was changed for all eternity.

About two-thirds of the team went home after the Sunday morning service feeling that God had concluded a good work. We, the remnant, came back at six o'clock and had a good service and were about to have the benediction. The pastor walked up on the stage to pray when a word came for him from the Lord. I rushed to prophesy on the piano and my friend sang the Word of the Lord to him.

A woman that we had ministered to off and on during the weekend had walked in from another church just as he started to give what we thought was the benediction. After the pastor's prophetic word, she took my place on the piano and began to play in the Spirit; the twelve-year-old grandson of the pastor ran to the drums; one of the ladies out of the congregation picked up the microphone and sang a prophetic song, "I am the weaver and you are my threads." It was like the Fourth of July fireworks at the finale when first one blast of fire goes off and then another until the sky is full of brilliant light.

Our ministry team went to the back of the sanctuary and watched a most miraculous move of the Spirit unfold. It was instant fruit. The entire congregation began to flow in and out of the prophetic song. All the people began to dance, jump, leap, and shout. They were waving streamers. The men were going everywhere with a sword. One of them would get up on the stage and enact the Word of the Lord with the sword and then another would come and exchange with him. The men formed a line and went all the way around the sanctuary shaking tambourines and colorful flags. All of this was happening spontaneously with no leader or encourager.

There was a little boy between seven and eleven with severe retardation. My minister friend took him by the hand and led him up on the stage. The woman was still playing the song of the Lord on the piano, the twelve-year-old boy still on the drums, and a fifteen-year-old boy that I had never seen before was playing on the synthesizer. Five teenage girls who had never danced spontaneously ran up onto the stage and began to dance before the Lord in unison with tambourines. My friend held the little boy to herself with one hand on his head. He put both arms around her waist. As she prophesied in song, the Lord sang to him, "You are My little man and you are an integral part of My end-time plan. You are an example of My mercy and grace and when people look at you they see My face."

The five little girls (nobody had told them what to do; none of them had ever danced before) formed a semi-circle around the little boy and began to shower him symbolically in a concentrated, choreographed movement that we all knew no one had ever taught them. They were showering him with glory and the love of the Lord, enacting visibly what the Lord was doing in the Spirit. The little boy wept and wept (and so did everyone else in the church).

I was sitting back there going absolutely crazy with excitement and joy. The momentum never stopped. It went on, one incredible situation right after the other. Another person out of the congregation came to the microphone and sang the Lord's words to the people, "You are My visage. You are who I am. You are the very expression of the great I Am." Words are so inadequate to express the enormity of what God was doing.

79

There was an old man in the sanctuary who was the first man to establish the church all those years ago, along with the pastor and had not been walking with the Lord closely for many years. He took the sword and started walking toward the stage. All the people in the church came with him up onto the stage, and held up his arms. A circle formed around him, and then another circle around that, and then another circle. And in the middle of all the circles the old man stood with his sword raised high and the people began to prophesy to the church. Prophetically, corporately and spontaneously, a congregation had formed (a wheel within a wheel) around the man who began the work with the Word of God (the sword) and blew the breath of life (prophesied to the dry bones) back into a dead body (the dying church). Our entire ministry team, totally uninvolved, was at the back of the church watching it happen.

We were seeing a prophetic enactment of the plowman overtaking the reaper. We saw life come out of death and rebellion (the teenagers from the street). We saw the Breath of Life minister to precious seed hidden from sight in forbidding-looking soil (the little boy). From the dead, not only did we see resurrection, but the entire cycle from plowing and planting and growing and harvesting to the baking of bread. These people moved instantly from a fallow field to the stage of baking bread to take to the nations.

Those are moments we store up and are encouraged by over and over again. It wasn't just a service where we had gone to teach and left in faith believing that transformation had taken place and fruit would come. We saw the transformation before we left. God has called every one of us to be a tiller of the soil, to be a husbandman, to be fashioned after the One Who created us—He Who has the heart of a plowman, Who has the heart for the earth, Who loves the earth. These moments the Plowman treasures in his heart forever.

HEART OF THE FATHER

I've been told that farmers love every part of the process. They like being out in the heat under the sun. They like using their muscles. They like the plow. They like the smell of the earth. They like sowing the seed. They like checking the fields and watching the little shoots come up. They like seeing the waving ears of corn. They like fighting all the worms and plucking the ears of corn. But that is something that God has to put in our hearts. We can't work that up. But we can allow God by an act of our will to so plow us up ourselves so that we receive that Father's heart.

I desire to speak from the heart of the Father. I don't want to just speak enticing words of men's wisdom. I don't wish to live out a sense of duty, just living the way that I know I should live as a Christian, or a minister or as a prophet. This is what a prophet does, this is what an apostle does, and this is what an evangelist does. That is putting the cart before the horse. I long to speak and proceed from the heart of the Father. We heard the heart of the Father over the little boy. I almost didn't survive the searing sweetness of that. That was amazing.

Plowing is not the purpose, planting is not the purpose, and even harvesting is not the purpose. The purpose is the seed. The plowman can't take any credit even though he is the one who does all the backbreaking work. The plowman gives the glory to the Lord because he knows that the life is in the seed. And God is the giver of life. It is the miracle of life that we are giving birth to as we plow, plant, and water. Much as Mary so long ago as a human vessel carried and gave birth to Jesus, so the plowing, planting, watering, the tilling, the fertilizing, and the growth—all is immaterial except God. God alone builds the house. Unless we realize and acknowledge that, we labor in vain.

We must learn the value of the seed, the importance of the seed, the miracle of the seed; we learn to recognize the miracle of life that is contained in the seed. If we keep our eyes on the work, the dirt, the filth, the frustration, and the agony (it's the agony and the ecstasy), then we have lost the vision that we are laboring to fulfill. When we get a revelation of the miraculous nature of the life that is contained inside of us which we have the ability to impart to others, then we realize the ecstasy and joy that sustains the heart of the plowman. The life of that seed is dependent not upon us but on the Father of all life, the giver of all good and perfect gifts. And He has put within us His heart—the heart of the Father of nations.

PROPHETIC PARABLE OF THE PLOWMEN

"For the season of accelerated growth is upon us, says the Lord. This is the age when we are past the slow unfolding of the seasons as the bright green shoots slowly push their way up through the earth, the robins are upon the grass and the rains water and the winds blow and the sun shines and slowly the plant, touched by the sun, begins to open until you have full flower. But this is the season of accelerated growth," says the Lord," this is the time when many seasons will be wrapped into one. And man will see many things which before would have taken several seasons for maturity, be born in a day, be born in an hour.

The acceleration process will be foreign to man's mind; it will be foreign even to the man who likes speed and instant success. For in the world of the unseen, where we look not at those things which are seen but at those things which are unseen, in that realm, man cannot comprehend speed in its proper connotation. Man likes the idea of the babies in Christ. He likes to feed the babies milk and change their diapers, because it makes him feel more mature. But the Eleventh Hour Workers who come upon the scene will be babies only for an instant. Accelerated growth will come, accelerated growth in the Spirit, where the plowman will overtake the reaper.

For a moment, meditate upon the plowmen of old. Further, meditate upon the mighty men of God who toiled by the sweat of their brow, men with callouses on their hands and muscles that strained against their garments, men that trudged endlessly down the fields row by row by row by row. It was slow and arduous labor. It was labor that often bore no fruit for many seasons. And as the plow pushed through the earth, the plowman would encounter obstacles, dead roots and stones, and the process would be halted while the obstacles were removed. But the plowman would go straight ahead, not veering to the left or to the right. He would go straight ahead no matter what obstacles were there.

The plowman rose early while even the birds were still asleep, and he worked until the light was gone. He lived close to the earth. He was in touch with it. He was in touch with the feel and the smell and the sight and the sound of the earth.

And as the plow pushed through the dirt, and the arduous labor trained muscles upon muscles, he would glory in the sun upon his back and the wind upon his face, in the songs of the birds and most of all, he would joy in the sight of the rows upon rows of freshly turned earth about to receive the seed, the seed of life, seed that would multiply and become food.

Food for the sower, food for the reaper and food for the plowman. And when the sun was gone and the plowman put his plow away for the night, he would go inside his house and before bed he would make music.

The plowmen of the Lord, men of music.

They were the ones who would reproduce the songs of the birds. They would reproduce the music in the wind, they would sing the lilt in the sky and rhythm was in their bones. And once the growth came and the field was filled with waving ears of corn, or with wheat, or barley, and the promise of bread was in the making, the work of the plowman was all but forgotten—forgotten in the exhilaration of the season of life.

But there were some plowmen who never saw the season of life, they never saw the field covered in grain, they never saw the reapers, they never saw the wheat as it was carried into the barn and laid upon the threshing floor. They never tasted the fruit; they never smelled the baking of the bread. Their life ended never knowing what the plow accomplished. Never knowing even the real purpose of the plow. For their vision was not beyond the field and the straight furrows of earth. But their vision was upon the next step ahead. Their vision was upon the next clod of earth to be broken and turned and tilled. They never looked beyond the task at hand.

Great concentration was required for this task of the plowman, for in many cases the ground was hard and fallow. The soil was crusted and hard. Many times the field that would become fertile with grain had been a forest, and there were more roots in the earth than there was earth. And though the plowman pressed and pushed and toiled because bread was required, many seasons of reaping were stolen. Stolen by the sky that would withhold the rain, stolen by the locusts and the pestilence and the plagues, stolen by dirt not fit to receive the seed, even after arduous plowing. Many plowmen labored through all the seasons in vain. Many of them died because of the lack of harvest, the very harvest that should have provided food for the plowmen. Blessed are those plowman/prophets who labored yet never themselves saw the fulfillment of the promise.

But many of the plowmen were also the harvesters and the reapers. Many of them did it all, says the Lord. They were content in the plowing because they knew the reaping would come. And to these plowmen, My sturdy plowmen, all seasons were alike. The thrill and the excitement of the freshly turned earth was just as exhilarating as the sound and the sight of the sickle as it cut through the golden wheat. The time of removing the stones from the pathway of the plow was the same as the time of carrying the wheat to the threshing floor. It was the same as the time of taking the grain to the baker. It was the same as the time of the smell of fresh bread. Because the plowman knew that the process was all one. The process of the plow and the sowing of the seed and the watering and the sunshine, the time of growth, the time of flowering and the bearing of the fruit, the time of harvesting, and the time of eating the fruit was all one, says the Lord. And now, and now, now in this place of time and dimension and space

now in this time of the hearing of My Word

where everything that I speak

might seem so absurd

now is the time of accelerated growth.

Now all of the seasons will happen at once. The time that the plowman will be overtaken by the reaper has come. But the function of both is important; now they will happen together. For one shall have a song and one shall have an exhortation and one shall have a prayer. One will plant and one will water and one will eat of the fruit. For in My kingdom, the plowman will work side by side with the reaper. In My kingdom, one man no longer has to do all things throughout the long and slow seasons. But I have multitudes, I have many parts of My Body. One wields the plow and one carries the seed, one swings the scythe, one grinds the grain and one bakes the bread.

So hear ye the parable of the plow, says the Lord. The most important part of the plow goes beneath the surface of the earth. It forges ahead in the darkness of the dust of the earth. It is sharp and hard and durable because it encounters many different challenges. But no matter what it encounters, it doesn't break, it doesn't bend, it doesn't shiver or shake. It is not fearful of what will happen in the darkness. It has a job to do. It is a hard job, it is an unlovely job, but the plow doesn't see it any differently than any other part of the process.

The blade, shining and glittering, cuts and divides the darkness from the light. Emotion doesn't enter into the process. Nor does understanding with the mind of man. Unprejudiced, impartial, and unafraid, the blade goes forward—never back. Cutting, piercing, jabbing, slicing, dividing, uprooting, turning, uncovering and covering, always moving, always effective, ever accomplishing its eternal purpose: the blade of the Word of the Most High God.

The plowman must believe in the effectiveness of the purpose of the blade. He must understand the ultimate necessity of the work of his tool, so that he can press on against all odds—in spite of the contrary rebellious nature of the dark sod. He must be ONE with his instrument, moving forward without deflection from his path. Only one purpose at a time, and that purpose is GOD'S.

His attention must at all times be on the business of the blade, lest the furrows of earth be crooked, or too deep, or too shallow, not ready for the seed. All is pointed toward the preciousness of the seed. Oh, that God's people would comprehend the remarkable nature, the infinite, eternal importance of the seed. All groaning, all travail, all the agony of birth, all the ceaseless labor of plowing, tilling, planting, and watering—all the work of wresting life from death, ALL is intrinsically inseparably linked to the protection, bringing forth, and ultimate flowering of the seed of God. The SEED."

V

THE SEED

Now may He who supplies seed to the sower, and bread for food, supply and multiply the seed you have sown and increase the fruits of your righteousness. 2 Cor. 9:10 NKJV

Central thought: As we progress from the milk of the Word to the meat, we are allowing that Seed of life full sway to flourish. We are becoming one, body, soul, and spirit with the Father and the Son (John 17), and the indwelling power of life will be all that we need. He is the vine and we are the branches. The source of life flows through the branches to the smallest leaf with no strain, no begging and pleading, and with unrestrained joy. Then we are truly fruit-bearing, seed-bearing, mature plants reproducing after God's DNA, and continuing the cycle of His supernatural Life.

PRINCIPLE OF THE SEED

The seed is the carrier of all life, and its sole function is TO PROPAGATE. Propagation is the innate nature of life. God's command, first to the earth (Gen. 1:11, 22), and then to the man whom He had created after His own Seed (Gen. 1:27-28), was to be fruitful and multiply. The wondrous earth created by the King of all creation was perfect, free of discord, death and disease. All seed reproducing after its own kind was also perfect. This harmony of nature was ruined and cursed after Adam separated himself from God by his disobedience, and we see the entrance of a disturbing seed different from God's lineage: the seed of the serpent.

And the Lord God said to the serpent, "Because you have done this, cursed are you more than all cattle, and more than every beast of the field; on your belly shall you go, and dust shall you eat all the days of your life; and I will put enmity between you and the woman, and between your seed and her seed; He shall bruise you on the head, and you shall bruise him on the heel." Gen. 3:14

Here is the famous Messianic promise that a Redeemer would rise up from the Seed of the woman. Though human and subject to the bruising of the serpent seed, He would be divinely begotten, and would crush forever the head of the serpent. To the end of the ages, the serpent seed would make war with the seed of the woman (Rev. 12:17), that massive company of Jesus' many brethren who overcome by the blood of that divine Lamb/Seed and the word of their testimony (Rev. 12:11).

And so began a divine and highly contested romance between the Seed of God and the seed of the woman, as we follow the line from Eve to Abraham. "And if ye be in Christ, then ye are Abraham's seed, and heirs according to the promise" (Gal. 3:29). The promise to Abraham was that his seed would be as numerous as the stars of the heavens. This seed led to the throne of David, and on to the Promised One, the Christ, the first-fruits of a many-membered nation.

We who are in Christ are born of divine, incorruptible Seed, a new race, a new breed, a royal priesthood and a holy nation. We, as seed, are reproducing after our own kind, our heavenly Father, the Father of all life. Even scientists will admit a great mystery: the essence of life is not in the natural seed, regardless of the kind or quality. Even the highest quality seed can rot, refusing to germinate. The true scientist would tell you that the life is in the DNA; the Spirit will tell you that it is the Breath of God. The miracle of increase inside each seed is God's and God's alone.

QUALITY OF LIFE IN THE SEED

In natural earth there are different qualities of seed, just as there are thousands, and even millions of different varieties of seed. Agronomists and horticulturists tell us of four kinds or qualities of seed. The first, foundation seed, is rare and the most precious of all seed. Scientists will tell you that foundation seed is pure in every sense and always breeds true. For example, red flowers with pink centers will always produce the same. This foundation seed is closely guarded and kept pampered; it is grown in a greenhouse and not available to everyone. It is only used to produce the first crop. Foundation seed determines the variety (contains the genetic characteristics) of all that is to follow it. It, the ORIGINAL seed, is too valuable to use all the time. Foundation seed is used to produce all other seed.

We can liken this foundation seed to God the Father, the Seed of life, the rarest and most precious of all seed, and the purest. The glory of God the Father is closely guarded in a secret and hidden place of great mystery—in a perfect environment. His only begotten Son, contains His exact "genetic" characteristics. "If you have seen Me, you have seen the Father" (John 14:9). He was the original Seed that was used for all the other seeds. The Seed is the word of God (Luke 8:11b). His Word, His Seed provides and creates the foundation of the existence of all things. Jesus is that foundation. "For by Him all things were created, both in the heavens and on earth, visible and invisible, whether thrones or dominions or rulers or authorities—all things have been created by Him and for Hi." (Col. 1:16). "For you have been born again not of seed which is perishable but imperishable, that is, through the living and abiding word of God" (1 Pet. 1:23). "In the exercise of His will He brought us forth by the word of truth, so that we might be, as it were, the first fruits among His creatures" (Jam. 1:18).

The second kind of seed in agronomy is certified seed. Certified seed is also rare and pure. It is grown in the field, however, rather than in greenhouses, and is produced from foundation seed by commercial seed producers. The name certified refers to the quality, the purity and the variety of the seed. It is guaranteed seed and grown to produce other seed.

Certified seed can be likened to Jesus Christ, the only begotten Son of the Father, and in us, that hope of glory. He came to earth (the field) as the first-born among many brethren—His purpose being to produce many others, the promised Seed of the woman. This certified Seed is also very costly, costing Him and us everything. Our lives are no longer our own, but we are bought with a price. He was the first fruits of a many-membered nation. With the Christ/Seed inside us, we are a part of that same crop, the certified seed coming directly from the Father. Commercial seed producers come into play as we view the five-fold ministry: apostles, prophets, pastors, evangelists, and teachers (Eph. 4:11), and to Bible schools and seminaries, who will encourage and teach us about this Seed. They plant and water, and God gives the increase.

The third kind of seed is field seed. Field seed comes from certified seed and is the third-generation seed. It produces the crop to be eaten. It is available to everyone, and is not the purest seed. Being grown in Farmer Brown's pasture, it can be greatly influenced by bees, insects, birds, winds and storms but can be planted again. And each time it is planted there is the possibility of losing some of the purity.

Field seed can be likened to the Word of the Father which we speak to one another and to the Body of Christ at large, and to the world. The seed is the Word of God (Luke 8:11), and the field is the world (Matt. 13:38). Field seed is a third-generation seed because it can be influenced so greatly by our natural mind, by our attitudes and traditions. The seed of the Word that we speak becomes field seed. It will produce a crop and it will be eaten by others. It is available to everyone, and we plant it again and again. But everywhere we go, we see field seed, the Words sown by those in the Kingdom, that contain weeds and tares and other elements that can cause that word to be just a little contaminated. It can become polluted by our tradition, or our hurts and wounds.

Have you ever seen a minister who has been greatly wounded, ministering out of his hurt? Ministering out of a wounded spirit is seed contaminated by the very thing ministers are committed to eradicating from the Body of Christ. This kind of field seed going out to the world will already carry within it an impurity, reproducing after its kind. Let us go back to our source. Let us go back to the certified seed which is Christ in us. Let us return to the foundation seed which is God the Father and let our field seed contain the highest percentage possible in this earthen vessel, full of purity and power.

The Seed

The last kind of seed is pasture mix. Pasture mix is a fourth-generation seed and depends totally on the current field. Made solely for animal consumption, it is not eaten by humans. Its original pure variety can no longer be identified. Pasture mix is seed that has grown up with too many weeds, contaminated seed with almost no purity.

In these last days there will be pasture mix passing for foundation and certified seed. Those whose motives have not been pure will speak out of that impurity, and deception will be generated. The Word warns us that in the last days even the elite will be deceived. Heresy will be rampant, bringing destruction and denial of the Truth, even while seeming to declare it.

> But false prophets also arose among the people, just as there will also be false teachers among you, who will secretly introduce destructive heresies, even denying the Master who bought them, bringing swift destruction upon themselves. 2 Pet. 2:1

> Then the Lord said to me, "The prophets are prophesying falsehood in My name. I have neither sent them nor commanded them nor spoken to them; they are prophesying to you a false vision, divination, futility and the deception of their own minds." Jer. 14:14

This contaminated, impure seed going forth will deceive great numbers of the Body of Christ. People who have allowed too many influences into their lives other than the Word of God will be teaching a mixture of truth and possible deception, and other doctrines than Christ (Eph.4:14). Groups we often identify as cults can grow out of this. The most frightening and powerful thing about cult doctrines is that they often contain a kernel of truth, usually surrounded by many lies (or weeds/ tares). It is often very difficult for the unsuspecting and the innocent who are truly seeking more of God to discern the difference. They see the kernel of truth and recognize it, and it blinds them to the lies.

In all four kinds of seeds, even in the natural, you can't tell by the outward appearance of the seed what kind of seed it is, or whether it will germinate. You can tell in some cases the variety of seed one from the other, such as wheat from oats, but not the quality of the seed. It is impossible to tell foundation seed from certified seed. Man looks upon the outward appearance but God the Father looks upon the heart.

In these last days it will be of paramount importance that we allow the laser light of the spirit of discernment to pierce directly to the heart so that we will carry pure seed to the fields. In these last days, God's sowers will carry the purest of all seeds ever known to man to the fields, seed which will germinate, bursting with life, and bear much fruit. The nations are our inheritance and God's inheritance, and He is sending us out to the fields to sow pure seed.

VARIETY OF THE SEED

The purest foundation seed is sown throughout the earth in millions of different varieties of plants, in flowering, fruit-bearing, nut-bearing and fragrance-wafting abundance. These seeds will vary in outward appearance. And so it is with us. In us is the pure Seed of Christ, but we are all unique and different varieties in God's garden.

Many who look upon the outward appearance will discern that if the majority of certain seed look one way, and one or two seeds look another, then the different seeds must be in some way inferior. Peer pressure is a powerful and often destructive force. As young children and teenagers growing up, it takes a great deal of courage to resist conformity. Peer pressure is a spirit which says you can't be different or you will be a freak. Conform to the gang if you want to be accepted. If everyone is wearing long full dresses and baggy pants, you can't wear straight skirts and dress pants. If everyone is wearing black leather jackets, you can't wear red plaid wool—not if you want to be popular.

Often in the fight to conform, the ultimate hidden truth is that in actuality you are conforming to rebellion. You may be conforming to a gang which is in total rebellion to all authority and even morality, but you ARE conforming. So we grow up spending our lives in misery, trying to make a pear tree bear persimmons. We must find out early how to accept what kind of plant we are. Are you a grape, or a fig? If we will only be content just to BE, and to be who we are and to grow happily where and how we are planted, we are agreeing with who the Father has created us to be. We will be secure in that knowledge.

Someday we may meet someone who bears the same variety of fruit that we do. Then we can happily compare how big it is and exactly what it tastes like and how many gallons the yield is and how much jelly we get each season. But once you get into comparisons, you may find that although we are the same kind of seed, the purpose is different. One may concentrate on fruit and jelly, while the other's focus is on the flower and the fragrance. How can a peach be jealous of a pear? All that God makes is good and perfect.

> For Thou didst form my inward parts; Thou didst weave me in my mother's womb. I will give thanks to Thee, for I am fearfully and wonderfully made; wonderful are Thy works, and my soul knows it very well. My frame was not hidden from Thee, when I was made in secret, and skillfully wrought in the depths of the earth. Thine eyes have seen my unformed substance; and in Thy book they were all written, the days that were ordained for me, when as yet there was not one of them. Psa. 139:13-16

It is not meant that you be a different creature than you are. There are ways that we can prune and fertilize and clean ourselves to become more like Him inside. It may take more water or more sun, or even the tree surgeon, but you are who He has made you to be. Even the hairs on our heads are numbered. Whether a rose or an oak tree or a grape vine, we are unique and precious in His sight.

The cactus is a funny little plant, so prickly and short and fat. But it can live a long time without water, and bears the most beautiful and exotic flowers. Cactus was made to live in special places. Unlike the cactus, "closet" plants are quiet and not spectacular, and yet they can grow in very dark places where not many can. We are not all created for the same purposes or to occupy the same space. But we are all created to be different, remarkable, and special parts of God's garden.

The eternal foundation seed and certified seed within us will always be pure and true to itself. Foundation or certified seed that produces a beautiful red flower with a yellow center will always produce a red flower with a yellow center, but that flower will fulfill a different purpose and have a different appearance according to the particular spot and purpose for which it is planted. The red flower may be placed in a window box in the middle of a city to bring refreshing in a place of concrete and heat. It will still be the red flower with the yellow center, but because of the unique surroundings, it will be viewed differently than others.

The red flower with the yellow center may be planted in an English garden surrounded by high brick walls and accompanied by saffron and cinnamon and fruit trees in abundance. The little red flower may not be as noticed here, because of the lushness of its companions. Because it is in a different place, a different kind of earth, it will affect our senses differently: but it will still be the red flower with the yellow center.

The red flower with the yellow center may be placed on a hillside, along a public highway, carefully landscaped for passing motorists. In this case, the red flower will have hundreds of brothers and sisters exactly like it except to the most experienced eye. The motorists will need masses of plants to appreciate the splashes of color as they go by at great speeds. So the little red flower will only be one of many. His individuality will not be noticed by the masses. But in symphony with all of his friends, he will bring great joy.

So there are many varieties of seeds, many hundreds and thousands of different kinds and varieties. Our purpose may be different. Our surroundings may be different, but we will all contribute to the overall joy of God's creation. One place and purpose will not be more important than the other, just different. The innate, eternal Seed is the same. Let us enjoy the variety of God's garden. Let us accept the uniqueness of each individual, as we look to that unchanging, unshakable pure foundation Seed within each vessel.

THE REMARKABLE NATURE OF THE SEED OF GOD IN US

We must allow God to bring us to the realization of the miraculous remarkable nature of that Seed which has been placed inside of us. Each seed reproducing after its own kind, we must understand that we are reproducing and being changed after the likeness of the Lord of Glory (Gen. 1:11-12, Gen. 1:24, Gen. 1:26).

Each seed is a miracle capsule that contains every element needed for the mature plant or tree or living creature. Within the acorn is an entire oak tree. Within us is all that God is. All of the authority and dominion given to Adam is ours. "And having summoned His twelve disciples, He gave them authority over unclean spirits, to cast them out, and to heal every kind of disease and every kind of sickness" (Matt. 10:1). Watching the nature of God develop within us is the most exciting miracle in life.

We must come to a realization of the magnitude of the amazing things that the Lord does through us: the fruits and the gifts of this Seed. How unusual and how supernatural the giftings of the Lord of Glory are: as sure and dependable as He is Himself, a precious treasure inside of us. For we have this treasure in earthen vessels to be valued, esteemed, protected, and used, just as Jesus Himself released the power of His Father (2 Cor. 4:6-7).

The acts and miracles that Jesus did were so much a part of Him and Who He was that there was no separation in Himself caused by doubt, hesitancy, or uncertainty. The word "confidence" means "firm belief, trust, reliance, assurance; being or feeling certain." When the mighty words "Lazarus, Come forth!" thundered through the air to the mouth of the cave, they were born upon the winds of complete assurance in the nature of their power. Let us be so irrevocably bound to the life of God inside us that we and the acts and miracles that Almighty God does at our hand are beyond thought, beyond doubt, and completely certain.

The mother and the unborn child within her are so at one that it is only with great ripping and tearing that the two are separated. We must become that aware of, and one with, the explosive and vast Being Who dwells inside of us. Women speak of post-partum depression, an empty feeling, a feeling of uselessness when the child is no longer inside the womb. The world today is driven by that very sense of emptiness and purposelessness. Many people spend great amounts of time and money trying to fill emptiness inside that only God can fill. We who have filled that God-shaped vacuum with the great Seed of Life can attain the same oneness with the Father of all life that Jesus had.

> That they may all be one; even as Thou, Father, art in Me, and I in Thee that they also may be in Us; that the world may believe that Thou didst send Me. And the glory which Thou hast given Me I have given to them; that they may be one, just as We are one; I in them, and Thou in Me, that they may be perfected in unity, that the world may know that Thou didst send Me, and didst love them, even as Thou didst love Me. John 17:21-23

In Jesus there was complete understanding of the greatness of the power which He carried. He said, "My hour has not yet come," aware of the importance of the timing of the unleashing of the power (John 2:4). We may doubt our ability to minister or flow in the spiritual gifts available to every believer, because we are still under the mistaken impression that we have something to do with it. The promise of God to Abraham that His seed would be as numerous as the stars of the heavens came long before the fulfillment of it. In fact, the Lord deliberately waited until there was absolutely no natural way for the promise to come to pass because of Sarah's age. But she conceived and the promise was fulfilled (Gen. 21:2).

True knowledge of the vast unknowable dimensions of the God we serve will produce patience as we work out our destiny. Line upon line, and precept upon precept, He is perfecting those things which concern us. His timetable may be a bit different than ours, but then He does not live in a time-space dimension.

Years ago, I had a dream in which I was given a precious treasure. This priceless gift was in the form of a gold clock whose chimes kept trying to go off at the wrong time. As the chimes went off they alerted certain unsavory elements wishing to steal the treasure. Finally, friends of mine took the clock with them for safe-keeping, and I understood that the clock would be restored to me at the appointed time when there was no longer any danger caused by running ahead of God's timetable.

RELEASING THE SEED

Jesus, unlike Abraham and Sarah, was completely aware and assured of the gift of God, the extent of it, the power of the appointed timing, and the incredible variety of the dispensation of it. The authority with which He spoke and ministered was often matched by the interesting ways in which He released it. God's plan and way is often incomprehensible to the mind of man. "But God has chosen the foolish things of the world to shame the wise, and God has chosen the weak things of the world to shame the things which are strong" (1 Cor. 1:27). Many times the miracle was released with only a word. Blind eyes were opened when He covered them with mud. Demons were sent forth from a man into a herd of swine. There were no formulas which the greedy mind of man can copy.

But Jesus never hesitated to answer the needy heart or body. He healed them all (Matt.12:15). We must, in recognizing the remarkable seed within, freely give that which has been given to us. So often we back away from releasing the gifts of God. We are shy, fearful of failure, unsure of the timing, and a hundred other excuses. A double-minded man is unstable in all of his ways (James 1:8). Wavering and hesitation has no place in the growth and release of the seed.

Releasing or imparting the miracle-working power of God often came with the laying on of hands. "And for this reason I remind you to kindle afresh the gift of God which is in you through the laying on of my hands" (2 Tim. 1:6). We find this word used in designating the gifts of the Spirit in 1 Cor. 12:4-10. The original Greek for "gifts" defines it as "extraordinary powers due to the power of divine grace operating by Holy Spirit." Jesus healed the sick as He "laid His hands on every one" (Luke 4:40).

Paul said, "But even if I am being poured out as a drink offering upon the sacrifice and service of your faith, I rejoice and share my joy with you all" (Phil. 2:17). Acknowledging the service to which we are called with joy and delight is to reaffirm with a resounding Amen! that very gift from the Father of Lights. We must never for one moment lose sight of the truth that we have absolutely nothing to do with the miraculous life and gifts inside of us—and therefore none of the responsibility of the outcome. God will do it His way and not ours.

Therefore, we must allow God to develop within us expectancy. Expecting always that God will use us to do the unbelievable, the unexpected, the miraculous, the unusual, and most particularly, the very things that we are personally incapable of. This expectancy is born of the knowledge that inside of us is the power that raised Jesus from the dead, the power that raised Lazarus from the dead, the source of the signs and wonders that turned water into wine. Inside of us is a fountain of supernatural, cataclysmic, miraculous, seismic, volcanic, atomic, nuclear power.

Each time that the Lord calls upon us to release that which He has placed inside of us, we must do it with the ease of an apple dropping off of an apple tree or a grape being plucked from the vine. We must allow the Lord to annihilate all fear, all discouragement and trepidation, that what we have inside us will not measure up, just not as good as what another has.

Can we not accept the spiritual truth that God has said in His word that every seed reproduces after its own kind, and that inside of us we have the same seed, the same quality of life that every great man and woman of God throughout the ages had in them. As God calls upon us to give a word of wisdom, or a word of knowledge, to prophesy, to heal the sick, raise the dead and cast out devils, let us look to the Lord of Glory and to that remarkable gift that we carry inside of us and let us EXPECT it to be released in all the fullness of God.

Let us just remember the joy of participating in God's harvest, participating with Him in the seasons of plowing and planting and sowing and reaping. In us is Christ the hope of glory, the hope of joy, and the hope of delight. In us it is the hope of deliverance, the hope of healing and salvation. In us is the hope of all that is infinite. All that He has asked of us is that we open our mouths and present our vessels as a living sacrifice, a living temple for the release of the Seed of God.

RELEASING SEED ON UNTILLED GROUND

In times past, there was so much emphasis placed on the importance of the seed, that there was little revelation regarding preparing the ground beforehand. The season of the great teacher, when the Lord restored that part of the five-fold ministry to the Body of Christ, was a great day of the propagation of the Word. But in many churches, the delivery of that Word was given paramount importance to the exclusion of all else, even while the delivery of the Word was orchestrated in certain and acceptable patterns. As a result, much seed was sown on ground that was ill-prepared, and in some cases not plowed at all. Many church services only had a token amount of praise and worship. The ground was not plowed and tilled and softened to receive the seed. Even the purest certified seed will eventually perish if the ground is not properly tilled and conditioned to receive it.

On the other hand, sometimes it seems in today's church services that we over-plow, causing the seed of the Word to take an inferior position in the service. The Body of Christ has been learning how to plow in praise and prepare the soil to receive the seed. As so often happens when God is restoring the revelation of a Truth to the Body of Christ, we go too far in that area. Finding the balance in all of the areas of our worship service can only come with God's wisdom and perspective.

But as we look with that fresh eye and perspective, we understand that the sowing of the Word doesn't always come in the form in which we are accustomed to receiving it. What might appear at first glance as over-plowing (too much praise) may be another thing altogether. The sowing of the Word cannot only come through the mouth of the preacher behind the pulpit in the designated part of the service.

The preaching of the Word can be done through the prophetic song. The preaching of the Word can go forth through enactments much as the prophets of old, in drama, mime and dance. The Word can go forth lifted up on a banner. Jesus was the Word made flesh, or visible. Soon He is coming in a form we may never have seen (Matt.14:25-26). So the Word is appearing in many different ways. Often we will finish a service and say, "But there wasn't any preaching. I'm hungry for the good old days when we used to value the Word of God. The Word has just taken a back seat." When in actuality, every action and every part of the service has been a sowing and a plowing and a reaping all at once: the plowman overtaking the reaper, and the remarkable Seed of God at the center of it all.

SEEDS OF DEATH AND DESTRUCTION

Pure seeds sown on even well-tilled soil may be joined, as they grow, by seeds less pure, seeds which will reveal their nature as they grow. Wheat and tares grow side by side in the field until the day they are divided, one for fruition and the other for destruction. Weeds and other undesirable elements spring up in our crop when man's perspective becomes clouded by unhealthy attitudes and perspectives.

It is unfortunate that dissatisfaction is so prevalent among us that it seems almost a trait inherent in the nature of man. It is like a blanket of thick glass that covers our ability to see. And though a man might be in extraordinary circumstances and stand upon the brink of unmentionable riches and wealth (whether spiritual or physical), if that spirit of dissatisfaction is like a colored blanket of glass over his eyes, he will not recognize the gifts and the riches that are laid out before him.

This is the day of breaking glass. This is the day of the smashing and shattering of so many of the different lenses that are worn over the eyes of the minds of the Body of Christ. And the shattering and breaking will be frightening, a fearful thing, much as removing dark glasses suddenly while in bright light. At first you can't see because the glare is so bright. The Body of Christ is on the brink of the time of great SEEING. But it must be preceded by a time of great shattering, because until the smoky glass is shattered, and the impaired vision is corrected and sharpened and focused, there will be no ability in the mind and the heart of man to proceed into the right direction (1 Cor. 13:12).

Dissatisfaction is sown like a tiny seed in a field of grain. Along with the wheat it gets watered, and along with the wheat it receives the sunshine, and along with the wheat it grows. But there will come a day of the separating of the grain from the surrounding weeds. Weeds that have grown from seeds of discontent, seeds of dissatisfaction, seeds of unfulfillment, will grow unnoticed until the day that the Lord brings them to light and the husbandman comes in to weed the field through deliverance, healing of emotions and renewal of vision. There may be many of those days in the development of our lives.

The plow can do its work and turn up dead roots and dead stones and turn over the earth and crust and mix up the salt and minerals and aerate the soil and homogenize it. The plow can do its work and seeds of life can be planted and covered over with that warm bed of earth. But even as the seeds of life begin to grow, other seeds can be brought in by the winds and storms, the birds, the fowl of the air, and grow right along with the seeds of life. Then the husbandman has another job, and that is to come along as the crop begins to grow, and to pull out by the roots those things that have grown from seeds of death.

We used to sing an old hymn about sowing. "Sowing in the morning, sowing seeds of kindness." As we go about our daily lives, our words are seeds. Our attitudes, actions, and our smiles, are seeds that are carried by the wind of the Spirit into the hearts of those around us. We have the ability to sow seeds of life and we have the ability to sow seeds of death that will get watered along with all the rest, and come up like weeds and tares among the crop.

When I am out in the early morning, walking and praying, and filling up my vessel with living water at the entrance of the day, I often pass strangers who are walking their dogs, and some probably doing just what I am doing. A smiling cheery "Good morning!" is a seed of joy. How often we can release seeds of joy into another's life free of charge, costing us nothing, not even much time. Just like the thrill of the bird's song at the dawning of the day can strike a chord of joy within our heart, so we have that same ability to impart seeds of life.

STRUCTURE OF THE SEED

Seeds of life released freely each day speak of a mature plant full of fruit which sheds its riches as an overflow from a vast inner supply (1 Cor. 3:1-3).

In the natural, seed is composed of two parts, the endoderm and the exoderm. The endoderm is the internal part of the seed which carries the life. In the beginning stages of development, the endoderm feeds on the exoderm as the seed sprouts internally and the root system is established—much as the fetus and the mother in pregnancy. As maturity comes and the plant grows, the outer covering of the seed is consumed. Soon the seed has become one with itself, growing and learning to reach out and incorporate the surrounding life-giving nourishment in broader spectrums. In maturity, the leafy parts of its own growth provide the plant with much of its required sustenance.

In like manner, as we put away jealousy and strife and all other fleshly attitudes, we allow our spirit to grow from the milk of the Word to the meat. We are decreasing and He is increasing. The old man is put away, and the nature of the divine Seed within takes over, spirit, soul, and body. We grow into another realm in God where spoon-feeding is no longer necessary. We have learned that Holy Spirit is the indwelling Spirit of Truth who will guide us into all truth. The river of life is inside of us, not forever on yonder shore.

As we progress from the milk of the Word to the meat, we allow the Seed of life full sway to flourish. We become one, body, soul, and spirit with the Father and the Son (John 17), and the indwelling power of life becomes all that we need. The more we grow, the more nourishment we will have available in our own "leafy" parts. He is the vine and we are the branches. The source of life flows through the branches to the smallest leaf with no strain, no begging and pleading, and with unrestrained joy. Then we are truly fruit-bearing, seed-bearing, mature plants reproducing after God's DNA, and continuing the cycle of His supernatural Life.

VI

THE SOWER

The sower sows the Word. Mark 4:14

Central thought: There are seeds which have been prepared since before the foundations of glory, waiting to be spoken. They are sitting and waiting in the vast storage areas of the hearts of God's people, waiting for the breath of God to blow them to the four corners of the earth. The seeds are alive and vibrant and glowing, of a vast profusion of different colors and shapes and sizes. The seeds sit and shimmer and pulsate with life, waiting to fill the hand of the sower. The Word of God will go forth out of the mouths of so many vibrantly different vessels, shooting forth like lightning bolts across the darkness of this present age.

PARABLE OF THE SOWER

And He spoke many things to them in parables, saying, "Behold, the sower went out to sow." Matt. 13:3

Any person can sow. Professional or amateur, strong or weak, rich or poor, young or old, any individual can plant seeds. A popular experiment in children's science classes when I was growing up was to plant seed in a shoe box and carefully note each day's progress. I can recall my investigation into the process of growing things. I remember going out into the back yard and digging up earth to carefully pack into the box. I went to the store to select my seed from among all the lushly colored paper seed packets, all gloriously advertising their flowering attributes on the cover. I put the seeds into the dirt with such hope and excitement, watering them according to my instructions.

I placed the box in the sunny window in the kitchen and breathlessly waited. I waited day, after day, after day, for some indication, some affirmation, that I had indeed done good and resourceful work. I waited in anticipation of the manifestation of the beautiful pictures on the seed packages. What I wanted was an instant garden. Of course, the seed grew incredibly slowly compared to the quality of my excitement. But being a child, my attention was quickly caught by other things. Then passing one day, I saw the first tiny green shoot peeking cautiously up through the soil. It was exciting to sow seed.

When Jesus told the multitudes the parable of the sower, His disciples asked Him why He had spoken in a parable. He answered, "Because it has been given to you to know the mysteries of the kingdom of heaven, but to them it has not been given" (Matt. 13:11). There is no greater seed ever to be planted than the message of the Kingdom of Heaven. It is a seed of faith, of hope and love; it is an eternal message of great joy. It is not just a seed that will rot in a bag in the hardware store waiting too long to be planted. The message of the Kingdom is not a natural seed. It is a supernatural seed. The sowers of the Kingdom are sowing supernatural seeds with the power to change lives for all eternity.

There are seeds which have been prepared since before the foundations of glory waiting to be spoken. They are sitting and waiting in the vast bins and storage areas of the hearts of God's people, waiting for the breath of God to blow them to the four corners of the earth. The seeds are alive and vibrant and glowing, of a vast profusion of different colors and shapes and sizes. And the seeds sit and shimmer and pulsate with life, and they wait to fill the hand of the sower. The Word of God will go forth out of the mouths of so many vibrantly different vessels, shooting forth like lightning bolts across the darkness of this present age.

VISION OF THE SOWER

And He was saying to them, "The harvest is plentiful, but the laborers are few; therefore beseech the Lord of the harvest to send out laborers into His harvest" (Luke 10:2). Responding to the call of the Father for sowers to labor in the fields requires longsighted vision seeing the field, the work, and the patience required. The sower needs a revelation of the preciousness of the seed which he carries in his bag, that his job might not be a wearisome task of simply casting forth a lifeless and insignificant grain of seed. His vision must be lifted beyond the furrows of prepared earth and the tiny seeds. His vision must see the seed as a finished crop. His vision must see in the seed the veritable world of life contained within each one. Seed would not be handled carelessly if all sowers had a revelation of the pulsating life within each tiny granule.

Just as that small child so long ago lost heart at the slowness of the growing of the seed, so mature sowers of the kingdom of God must take courage and not measure things by first appearances. The smallest seed, which is eternal, is so far beyond any natural thing in power and capacity, no matter how large it might seem. God can greatly multiply seemingly insignificant beginnings and use them as matters of global importance.

> He presented another parable to them, saying, "The kingdom of heaven is like a mustard seed, which a man took and sowed in his field; and this is smaller than all other seeds; but when it is full grown, it is larger than the garden plants, and becomes a tree, so that the birds of the air come and nest in its branches."
> Matt. 13:31-32

I remember that the wonder and delight in watching the plant grow from the seed which I had sown lay in knowing that it seemed to have a life all its own. Just as that seed grew as a miracle out of the depths of the earth, so the seeds that the sower of the kingdom sows are totally outside his control. From such a tiny seed, hardly big enough to notice, comes the tall stately tree. The source of such expansion is supernatural. The increase of the kingdom and the fruit thereof is God's part of the plan (1 Cor. 3:6).

And in that day I will respond, says the Lord; I will respond to the heavens [which ask for rain to pour on the earth], and they shall respond to the earth [which begs for the rain it needs],

And the earth shall respond to the grain and the wine and the oil [which beseech it to bring them forth], and these shall respond to Jezreel [restored Israel, who prays for a supply of them].

And I will sow her for Myself anew in the land, and I will have love, pity, and mercy for her who had not obtained love, pity, and mercy; and I will say to those who were not My people, You are My people, and they shall say, You are my God.
Hosea 2:21-23 AMP

When God the sower prepared the world as His field, He watched in all of His infinite patience, omniscience, and omnipotence as His vast plan unfolded through all the long ages. He patiently plowed a people rebellious and hard of heart to receive the most precious, the rarest, indeed, the only Seed around which the ages revolved. He gave this most precious of gifts and watched Him fall into the earth and die, that curses and plagues and pestilence might be removed from His Garden.

"I will sow her for Myself." The everlasting Father sowed into the earth His very Life's blood, and all creation groans in travail for the manifestation of the sons of God. Listen to the earth. Hear the corn and wine and oil. Hear the cry of the Lord's creation as His Word manifests in the earth. His Word cries out to be born in all creation like a child crying in its mother's womb. The birth of the Man-Child from the Seed of God and the Seed of the woman brings a new genus, a new species, a new creature, a new earth and a new heaven. The progeny from the marriage chamber of the Lamb is the shout of the Voice of the Lord answering Himself. God's answer to God. "LET US CREATE IN OUR OWN IMAGE!"

That great shout of the Lord as He sowed into the earth—and continues to sow—has caused the earth to answer with life: with grain, new wine and oil. Life has triumphed over death, and His plan is still unfolding, flowering through the Seed of the woman, His wondrous Garden, the Church.

So the Body of Christ, Jesus within being the Head, continues to plow the great field of the world. The Father has given the Church the nations for its inheritance, and together we go out to the vineyards and the fields laboring and bringing in His rich harvest. It is together in labor with Him that we are brought into even greater depths of His love.

> Come, my beloved, let us go forth to the field; let us lodge in the villages. Let us get up early to the vineyards; let us see if the vine has budded, whether the grape blossoms are open, and the pomegranates are in bloom. There I will give you my love.
> Song 7:11-12

The vision of the sower must reach the Father's perspective in order to comprehend the great principle of sowing, set into operation in the foundations of glory. Too often as we labor in the fields, preaching and teaching the Word, sowing the seeds of the Kingdom, we are discouraged by lack of fruit. We weep in despair when no one responds to an invitation or an altar call. We watch the faces of the people in the congregation and we are encouraged when they show positive response or encouragement. We are discouraged when they fold their arms and sit back, showing by their body language resistance or disapproval.

Our eyes and attention have been deflected from the Lord of the Harvest and His great love to the vines, the plants and soil. In actuality, we have allowed the hardness of the earth to cause discouragement for the plowman. We have allowed the slowness of the development of the seed to cause despair and apathy in the sower. Our faith is in the perverse and fickle nature of the earth rather than in our unchangeable and unshakable Partner: the King of all.

Keeping the King's perspective in all things is a challenge. The sower must be led of the Spirit in the variety of seed that he carries to each particular field. In the natural field, the furrows prepared for wheat may differ from the furrows prepared to receive potatoes or corn or olive trees. Reception of the seed, and the resulting fruition, will be greatly affected by the anointing of an apple of gold in a setting of silver (Prov.25:11). As we prepare to go, we must seek the Lord for the "word in season," a vital part of our preparation.

God's end-time sowers are "visionaries," looking beyond the task at hand into the shining of His face. In beholding Him and becoming like Him, His wisdom and His omniscience are the stay, guide and light upon the path ahead. The vision of the sower encompasses not only the field at hand, but embraces the fullness of God's vast plan. The sower recognizes that he is only a part of the plan and answer of God's great Spirit as He sows Himself into His earth.

SOWING IN TEARS

> Those who sow in tears shall reap in joy. He who continually goes forth weeping, bearing seed for sowing, shall doubtless come again with rejoicing, bringing his sheaves with him.
> Psa. 126:5-6 NKJV

The job of the husbandman can be a difficult one, as he juggles the need to sow the right seed, the problems of the field, the conflicting seasons, and the opposition to his work with his own personal life, health, and well-being. He himself as the plowman is at the same time being plowed. He also has roots and stones and thorns in his life which must be dealt with and destroyed (2 Kings 20:5). Many times, instead of attending someone else, what he really wants and needs is to be attended to himself. While sowing seed in the fields, he himself has need of fresh seed. And with the mercy of the Lord at work in his life, he too often takes the sorrows of those around him to himself (John 11:34-36). Jesus was a man of sorrows and acquainted with grief (Isa. 53:3).

Often the Lord calls upon us to go forth carrying His precious seed in the midst of personal tragedy. These are times when "sowing in tears" has an especially deep and profound meaning in our lives. My precious and only sister went to be with the Lord at an earlier age than those of us who were left would have desired. Many months before I had scheduled a conference on the weekend that her final memorial service was set. When the crises came, I sought the Lord about changing my plans, and He directed me to cancel the bulk of the weekend conference, but to continue with the Friday night service (which was in another state) before her memorial service on Saturday morning.

So my husband drove me three hundred miles into the neighboring state where I preached, ministered and prophesied healing, deliverance and joy to God's people. Leaving there at midnight, I arrived in Louisiana at four-thirty Saturday morning before the service for my sister at ten, where I sang and ministered. My soul was distressed and grieving, my physical body was exhausted, but after ministering to God's people I then ministered to my family.

The old song says, "In times like these, we need a Savior; in times like these, we need an anchor." In those times I did indeed need to put down my root deep into the love of God, that what I ministered would be the word of life, hope and joy needed by God's people, not influenced by my own human grief and loss. In my heart I delivered my sister into the hands of my eternal Father, trusting that He had taken her into fields of even greater harvest.

Charles H. Spurgeon called the ministry of tears "liquid prayer." The tears of humility and brokenness of the laborer in the field of personal broken dreams produces a harvest of rejoicing. Jeremiah, often known as "the weeping prophet," sowed seeds of repentance in the midst of a violent and dark period in the history of God's people. His personal life was a sacrifice upon the altar of the delivery of God's Word. Jeremiah's words are known for their poetry and lyricism, even while they cut with the sharp sword of judgment which leads to repentance. He truly was one who went forth weeping while bearing his seed. His empathy and love for the earth into which he was given to sow caused tears of compassion even as he suffered at their hands.

Though surrounded by peril and persecution because of the Word he spoke, still Jeremiah said, "His Word was in my heart like a burning fire shut up in my bones; I was weary of holding it back, and I could not" (Jer. 20:9, NKJV). Just as Jeremiah walked amidst danger and cruel opposition, so we must know the wiles of our enemy who is like a roaring lion, seeking whom he may devour. He, too, stalks the land in order to sow.

Once I was visiting a museum with my husband when we came across a riveting and most thought-provoking painting entitled, "The Sowers." Painted by Thomas Hart Benton in 1942, the picture depicts laborers sowing heads of skeletons into a bloody field with hands of death. The world was at that time being torn asunder by World War II, and death was reaping the whirlwind all across our sphere.

Underneath the painting he had written these words, "Are we to stand by and let them reap? These sowers of death, bloated with their gorge of human blood, are right now marching over the curve of the earth straight toward us, leaving fires of destruction in every furrow of the lands they traverse. They will not be halted by our refusing to see them nor will they be softened by cajoleries of appeasement. They want what we have and with their brigands they will take it unless we can find again some of the iron that was in the souls of our fighting forefathers."

Marching over the curve of the earth today are the same harbingers of death. They may appear in different forms, and manifest new strategy, but nonetheless, they are here. Side by side in the same field as the sowers of life, they tirelessly move forward with their plan. In the midst of plowing, sowing, and harvesting, we also find ourselves in the midst of battle. In ages past, those servants in desperate situations and desperate battles went to the Lord in fastings and tears even while the hand of the Lord continued in His plan of deliverance (Esther 4:1,3). We have need for patience and trust. Armor is imperative.

But above all, perseverance is most crucial. The task often seems impossible. Overwhelming. And the Lord gently reminds us, "Preach the word; be ready in season and out of season; reprove, rebuke, exhort, with great patience and instruction" (2 Tim. 4:2). We must be ready to sow no matter the season, no matter the circumstance, no matter our personal state of feeling. The mouthpiece of God is a vessel which goes whithersoever the Lamb should lead, always ready to sow that Word which will go forth and fulfill its own purpose.

In your faith supply moral excellence. And in your self-control, perseverance. And in your godliness, brotherly kindness, and in your brotherly kindness, love. For if these qualities are yours and are increasing, they render you neither useless nor unfruitful in the true knowledge of our Lord Jesus Christ. 2 Pet. 1:5-8

THE ELIJAH GENERATION OF SOWERS

As he applies these attributes, the sower of the Word of God is part of an end-time prophetic Elijah generation that will create with the great Creator by the power of the Word. Whether through the anointed preaching of the Word, the power of prophecy, the written Word in books, pamphlets, and magazines, or through music, the seeding of the Word will bring death to life before our very eyes. The Word of the kingdom will go forth through the mouth of the prophets with the same power that brought forth light in the beginning, and resurrection life out of death. Psalm 29 is a powerful example of the praise of the saints and the resulting outpouring of the Voice, the Word, the Seed of the Lord.

Ascribe to the Lord, O sons of the mighty, ascribe to the Lord glory and strength. Ascribe to the Lord the glory due to His name; worship the Lord in holy array. Psa. 29:1-2

As the plow of the Lord goes forth in praise and we magnify and lift up the Name of Jesus, His voice (the voice of Jesus, the Bridegroom) is heard in the midst of the congregation. "I will proclaim Thy name to My brethren, in the midst of the congregation I will sing Thy praise" (Heb. 2:12). This statement is made by Jesus, the Lord of the Harvest.

As worship goes forth and we seed the clouds with the moisture of living water, the heavens release that same Presence of the Most High God upon the congregation, and the circle of life-flow liberates the voice of the Lord through the mouths of His worshippers in prophetic flow. The singers will sing it (Psa.40:3), the players on instruments will prophesy it (2 Chron. 29:27), dancers and dramatists will enact it (Psa.149:3, Hosea 12:10, AMP), banners will proclaim it (Ps. 20:5), preachers will declare it, and all together in unity, the congregation will become in Truth that prophetic generation "seeing" into the realm of the Spirit and manifesting what they see—in earth as it is in heaven!

The voice of the Lord is upon the waters; the God of glory thunders, the Lord is over many waters. Psa. 29:3

The voice of the Lord Jesus is multiplied through His Body, the corporate many-membered Son. The voice of the Lord is like the sound of many waters (Rev. 1:15). Out of our belly flows rivers of living waters (John 7:38). The voice of many waters is us! That voice of thunder is the thundering of the voices of God's people, His sowers, vessels of honor, releasing His power out of their midst, sowing the seed of His Word!

The voice of the Lord is powerful. Psa. 29:4a

As I began to be used of the Lord in prophetic ministry to the Body of Christ (Acts 21:9), I was amazed by the sheer dominion, authority and might of the Voice of the Lord. Early on, I learned to prophesy to the seed, not the dirt. The voice of the Lord encourages the seed to grow rather than emphasizing the dirt, the sin or the negative character. So often the frailties and weaknesses of the dirt can be overwhelming, but as we keep our inner eyes upon the seed of God, He directs His voice to that part of the person like Himself. Then as the seed grows it pushes away the dirt.

One Sunday morning I prophesied to a man I had thought of as a leader in the church, and the Lord spoke to him powerfully about being a paymaster in the Kingdom. God told the man of the large amounts of money that God would cause to pass through his hands to bless the Body of Christ, and ended by saying that the man would move in signs, wonders, and miracles. It was evident by the man's outer reaction that the Lord had spoken to a deep place within, and he wept. In the evening service that same man ran down the aisle, bringing his whiskey bottle to lay at the altar. Unknown to most of us, he had been an alcoholic for many years, and the power of the prophetic voice had seeded him with repentance, birthing the strength within to become free.

Often when I prophesy, I watch people begin to waver as the Word goes forth, much like those in the movies who are being shot with a gun. They will stagger back and forth in waves without being touched, until the Spirit of the Lord has so overcome their flesh that they can no longer stand.

Many of these receive the rest of God's Word to them while "resting before Him" on the floor.

The voice of the Lord is majestic. Psa. 29:4b

Along with His power, God's people are discovering His majesty in these last days. Writers are breaking forth on the horizon with pens of fire. Singers are pouring forth prophetic songs from the heart of the King. The majesty and splendor of the Lord is being revealed in sharp words clothed in elegant imagery. The day of enticing words of men's wisdom will give way to a new day bursting with light and fire and brilliance. The Seed of the Word will drip with the revelation of the beauty of our God.

The voice of the Lord breaks the cedars; yes, the Lord breaks in pieces the cedars of Lebanon. Psa. 29:5

The awesome force of the storm in nature suggests the explosive power of the Word of God. The cedars of Lebanon in scripture were the mightiest tree known at that time. Towering and strong, they were used for coffins and other purposes requiring strength and longevity. That the voice of the Lord has the ability to break in pieces such strength indicates a power so vast that the mind of man can only wonder at it. The cedar can represent the forces of darkness and adversity that seem so overwhelming. It can also refer to the places within each of us which need to be broken and humbled by the plow of God to prepare a fit vessel for the seed.

I was ministering in an altar call one evening in a certain city, when I came to a woman who, at my first gentle touch, immediately shrieked, fell on the floor and began to writhe and foam at the mouth, all the while emitting ear-splitting shrieks. Friends of our ministry team were in attendance, who had brought with them a pastor who did not believe in casting out devils. He happened to be seated just beside where the woman fell. I knelt beside her (and also beside him) and tried to cast out quite a number of spirits, with no visible success.

Finally in desperation, I called out to the Lord in my spirit, "Help me!" The Lord spoke one word quietly to my inner self. "Prophesy!" At this point, I would have tried anything! I began to prophesy to the still violent woman. What happened was an amazing thing. I will remember this as one of the most valuable lessons I have ever learned. By the spirit, I saw demons begin to fly off of her. At the end of the prophecy, she sat up, in her right mind, with a sweet smile on her face. Her entire countenance was changed. The vast power of the voice of the Lord had broken in pieces the giant cedars in her life, stripping away the chaff, and freeing His Seed within her to rejoice.

> And He makes Lebanon skip like a calf, and Sirion like a young wild ox. Psa. 29:6

Have you ever noticed a puppy or a young colt, frisking out in the open, jumping from place to place out of the sheer energy and joy of life? The Hebrew word for "skip" means "leap for joy, dance." The word "Lebanon" refers to purity, and the word "Sirion" means "coat of mail, breastplate, covered with armor." The righteousness and power of the people of God in the last days will be born, not out of law, duty or the arm of flesh, but upon the wings of dancing, laughter and joy in the Holy Spirit. The voice of the Lord has the ability to release such laughter and exhilaration that God's people will be strengthened beyond strength. "Blessed is the man whose strength is in Thee. They go from strength to strength, every one of them appears before God in Zion" (Psa. 84:5,7).

One of the most memorable displays of God's sovereign joy occurred when my minister friend and I were serving in a country which was still overcoming years of deprivation, suppression and oppression. The women, in particular, were bowed down and walked on the streets without making eye contact. On the last day the pastor of this particular church had requested that we do a women's meeting. When we prayed, the Lord instructed us to teach on joy.

We began, not able to comprehend what could possibly happen in such a depressed atmosphere. While we were still teaching, the joy of the Lord hit the women. They were unfamiliar with the sensations as they tried to hold their mouths to keep the bubbles of joy from releasing. Giggles began to break out. Actual laughter escaped from first one and then another. They began to bend over with the force of the joy. Those containing it and still watching were soon infected and they began to fall out of their chairs. One woman rolled and laughed uncontrollably for some time. We found out later that she was scheduled for surgery the next morning. When she arrived at the hospital they discovered in pre-surgery tests that the problem was gone and there was no need for surgery. Another woman came and said that she had never laughed in her life before this day. Another said I did not know it was possible to laugh like that.

Through us God sowed seeds of joy, breaking the oppression of a lifetime in moments. Our God is a God of joy! He is our song! He is our deliverer and the lifter of our heads! He will cause us to skip with joy, His joy!

The voice of the Lord hews out flames of fire. Psa. 29:7

The Lord, by the power of His Word, is creating a "People of Fire." (I refer you to the author's book *Flaming Purpose*.) These flaming saints will be carriers of His light, His fire, veritable lightning bolts of the Presence and power of Jehovah. "Then the Lord will appear over them, and His arrow will go forth like lightning; and the Lord God will blow the trumpet, and will march in the storm winds of the south" (Zech. 9:14). "And of the angels He says, "Who makes His angels winds, and His ministers a flame of fire" (Heb.1:7).

We are entering the Day of the Lord. The prophets often used the storm with all of its fury, thunders and lightning flashes to paint a verbal picture of the Day of the Lord. We, as flaming ministers, as plowmen and sowers and harvesters of the army of light, are a part of that storm. We will march in those stormy winds and the trumpet will make its voice heard through us. And His voice, the Seed of His Word, will divide, hew out and shall cut asunder the blazes of lightning.

Once in the midst of intercession with friends I had a vision. As we prayed, I saw that I was standing on the earth with my feet spread wide and my face lifted toward the sky. Then lightning came from heaven and hit my head and went through my body, through both legs and feet and into the ground. I knew that the lightnings of God's power were flowing through us and into the region in our intercession.

> The voice of the Lord shakes the wilderness; the Lord shakes the wilderness of Kadesh. Psa. 29:8

This is the day when everything which can be shaken will be shaken. The wildernesses in our lives, the places of dryness, lack of fruition, the places of rebellion and defiance will be shaken and torn asunder so that the wilderness might be made a place of springs. The voice of the Lord is not always a popular voice. As a result, the prophets of old sometimes ran from the Lord and the Word given them to deliver. The Word of God will pierce as a sharp sword, cleaving and dividing the wheat from the chaff in our lives. The literal meaning of the Hebrew word for "shakes" is "to twist or whirl; dance; writhe in pain; to wait." There is travail and a birthing which takes place at the sound of His voice, a sound which ALWAYS impregnates.

> The voice of the Lord makes the deer to calve, and strips the forests bare, and in His temple everything says, "Glory." Psa. 29:9

The creative Voice that seeded the world in creation causes birth to come. Out of death, pain, and travail, the Word of the Lord brings life and resurrection. His power can strip away the false coverings, laying open all that would be hidden. At the splendor of such power, the only response of His Holy Ones, those Sons of the living God who are His temple, is to cry, "Glory!"

> The Lord sat as King at the flood; yes, the Lord sits as King forever. The Lord will give strength to His people; the Lord will bless His people with peace. Psa. 29:10-11

The King of all creation who sat above the deluge even now sits enthroned above all circumstance, all would-be powers, and all peoples great and small. The word "forever" means "to veil from sight." Even though we do not see clearly in this present age, far beyond what any man can see or even imagine, the Lord reigns as King. Jesus, Who is our living peace (Eph. 2:14), has brought all of us into union with the triune, invisible God. As branches of that eternal Vine, we simply receive the flow of strength, peace and power through our very veins: King's kids!

SOWING IN VAIN

It is painful for us to note in these last days in the Body of Christ, many are sowing, not to the kingdom of God, but to their own kingdom. Whatever is sown is also reaped (Gal.6:7). In building a house for our own purposes, our own ambitions, and our own desires, we neglect the building of the temple of the Most High God. The people in Haggai's time had returned to their homeland to rebuild the temple of the Lord. After a good start, construction ceased as opposition came, discouragement and apathy set in, and dissatisfaction concerning their circumstances deflected their attention from their true purpose. The Lord sent in the prophets with a strong message to consider their ways and to apply themselves to the house of the Lord (Haggai 1:4-7).

Sowing in other than God's fields can reap trouble and iniquity (Job 4:8). Those who stray from the path of the Lord's call often begin by taking just one step off the main thoroughfare in the interests of "vision." And as they pride themselves on being visionaries, they begin to see visions out of their own mind, rather than out of the Word of God.

"He who observes the wind will not sow" (Eccl.11:4). In these last days as the whirlwinds of an end-time storm toss us to and fro, it behooves us to earnestly remember the Lord in the night seasons, and to carefully consider our ways, lest we sow for ourselves a crop of judgment. "For thus says the Lord of Hosts, 'Once more in a little while, I am going to shake the heavens and the earth, the sea also and the dry land. The latter glory of this house will be greater than the former,' says the Lord of hosts, 'and in this place I shall give peace,' declares the Lord of Hosts" (Haggai 2:7,9).

As we continue to bring our aim and attention back to the message of the Kingdom of Heaven, sowing to His temple and building His kingdom rather than our own, we will not sow in vain. We will prepare that eternal dwelling that He might fill it according to His Word with His glory—seeds sown on good, fruitful and productive soil.

SOWING IN GOOD SOIL

As sowers of the Word, we carefully seek the Lord in choosing which fields to till and work. No one comes but the Father draw him (John 6:44). Sowing foundation seed in an improper environment is a waste of seed. "Do not give what is holy to dogs, and do not throw your pearls before swine, lest they trample them under their feet, and turn and tear you to pieces" (Matt. 7:6). The Lord chooses the field and then sends the laborers. If the sower sows only in the field where God sends him, the Spirit will join us in plowing the soil, preparing the ground, and sowing into fertile, hungry fields.

There is a people of good soil in these last days prepared by the Father with a hunger burning deep inside their innermost being for the King. He sends the sower out to these fields bearing life-giving, life-changing seed, all the while carrying within himself the strength and peace of the King. "It was planted in good soil beside abundant waters, that it might yield branches and bear fruit, and become a splendid vine" (Eze. 17:8). Let us look for the good soil as He leads us, producing a hundred-fold (Matt. 13:8, Luke 8:8)!

As the sower follows the path set for him by the Most High God, his steps and his path will be suffused with light and joy, and the seeds which he is carrying will pulsate with their light and with their life as they fall into the darkness of the earth. He will walk his path with jubilation in the knowledge that the light and the living water will bring forth that transformation needed for a new creation. As the sower goes forth to good soil, he can be confident that God the Father has gone before, plowing and tilling the soil, and teaching it to receive the seed.

Many people have been buffeted and bruised and battered by the storms of life. They have been so torn and wounded by the sticks and stones and enemies in the darkness that they have withdrawn. They have lost the ability to trust. They are only aware of the pain in life, having lost the ability to discern that in receiving life, their emotions will gain the ability to discern the joy, delight and pleasures and tastings of their God until his is the only voice they hear.

The call of the Lord has gone out to the ends of the earth for laborers who will go to the fields, preparing the earth to receive the Seed of life. Those who have become hard, distrustful, and rebellious toward the Seed must learn the power of light to destroy their darkness. As they learn to open themselves to the new Word of the Lord and the work of His plow, trust will grow in His ways. Gradually they learn that receiving the Seed is necessary for transformation to occur. The transforming power of the God of all life releases a life-flow whereby those once bound in darkness not only receive the Seed, but become one with it, becoming the sower themselves, and the plowman, and the harvester. They have become one with the exciting, enervating and joyous cycle of His life. Having been taught to receive, they have chosen to become good soil. They have chosen LIFE.

> And the seed in the good soil, these are the ones who have heard
> the word in an honest and good heart, and hold it fast, and bear
> fruit with perseverance. Luke 8:15

Receiving the seed sometimes seems easier when it comes in the form of formal teaching than when it is released in prophetic flow. But what we recognize as a prophetic word spoken into our lives demands a response. In times past there have been many "responses." Outrage. Unbelief. Skepticism. Or, on the contrary, a push to run out and bring it to pass. What is the balance and the proper scriptural response? An honest and good heart, good soil, will earnestly hold fast to the precious counsel of the Holy Spirit, our inward witness and confirmation.

With that witness in mind, we "make war with the prophecies" we have received (1 Tim. 1:18). A friend of mine received revelation from the Lord concerning the prophetic word she had received. The Lord showed her that the prophetic word spoken over her is like "heavenly currency." As she receives that Word from the Lord, she then returns it to Him in prayer and faith, exchanging that "currency" for the manifestation of the thing which was prophesied.

Certainly that same faith is required for the sower himself, as he is the caretaker, the guardian, the dispenser of words of such power (Rom. 12:6).

Faith is required for the sower to scoop up the seeds of life. Faith is required for the sower to make his way to the right field. Faith is required to sow with his eye upon a plentiful harvest. Faith is required by the earth to receive the seed with joy, to gently caress and comfort the seed as it begins to burst into new life.

Faith is required for those who come to water, to fertilize and encourage the new growth. Faith is required for those who would come to care, cultivate and till as the crop matures. But this faith is not the blind faith of one who hopes against hope. This faith is the God-given ability to know from a finished perspective that the crop is harvested even before the seed was sown. The joy that sowing seed in good soil brings undergirds and uplifts the farmer and strengthens and broadens his vision to expand more, expect more, and reap more abundantly.

REAPING IN JOY

> Those who sow in tears shall reap with joyful shouting. He who goes to and fro weeping, carrying his bag of seed, Shall indeed come again with a shout of joy, bringing his sheaves with him. Psa. 126:5-6

So leap forth into joy, all you sowers of the Word, all you men and women of God who have been called out of darkness to dip your hands into the words of light and life and to carry the pulsating vibrating seeds of life to a dark and an unknown earth. Strengthen yourself with power in your inner man, as the Lord calls forth the sowers into the fields. Set your eyes upon the seed with a fresh view, with a fresh gaze, knowing and understanding the value of the life that is contained there. Count not the steps, the labor or the time. But count it all joy, knowing that in sowing, you are also reaping words of life. An old hymn says it well:

> *Sing them over again to me*
> *Wonderful Words of life!*
> *Let me more of their beauty see*
> *Wonderful Words of life!*

The Sower

The joy of the Lord provides the strength for the hard labor of the husbandman. Joy is the skip in the step and the lilt in the voice that makes receiving the seed irresistible. Joy is the quality of life that brings healing to the bones. Joy is the melody in the song behind the dancing hearts of God's people. Joy is the music that sings in the veins, unspeakable and full of glory. Joy is the sound from heaven that breathes of God's grandeur. Joy is the audible expression of the colors and the brilliance and the vibrant splendor of the King.

Joy is the birdsong at first light and the call of the thrush and the nightingale and the creatures of the field in the darkness. Joy is the sight of the shinings in the heavenlies beyond the feel and the smell of the despair of this world. Joy unites us all in a common love, a common purpose and a common destiny. Joy is that which provides the impulse to put one step in front of the other, laugh while we do it, and applaud as the trials go past. Joy is the fresh smell of rain in the air that will cause the peoples of the world to cry out, to hunger for, to desire, and to long for the receiving of the seed from the hand of the Sower.

VII

POURING OUT

And behold, the glory of the God of Israel was coming from the way of the east. And His voice was like the sound of many waters; and the earth shone with His glory. Eze. 43:2

Central thought: The voice of the Lord is like the sound of many waters. The many waters are the streams flowing from the corporate, many-membered Son, the Body of Christ. And this is the plan fulfilled: that all the earth will be filled with the glory of the Lord as the waters cover the sea. The river of God freely flowing out of its earthen banks will bring glory, healing and life to all the earth, seeding it unto harvest.

PRINCIPLE OF POURING OUT

Have you ever stood at the window on one of those dark and windless days when the rain comes down as though it has been poured out of some vast, eternal bucket? It falls in such an unmeasured, relentless flow that it thunders into the earth and you wonder where it can all go, that surely the heavens will run dry of it soon. But the skies never seem to tire of releasing their endless burden, and soon you tire and retire to a book or a nice cheery fire.

Or have you ever sat on a huge boulder at the foot of an immense waterfall, near enough to feel occasional spray, gazing at the towering column of raging water and wondering what dry place has been left—once all those tons of water have deserted it for more favored climes? Or in the midst of a hurricane, have you watched angry tidal waves batter the coast with frightening power so out of control of all of man's extensive and clever scientific wonders?

Even in nature, we see the display of God's power and the immensity of His vast ability, and yes, even His willingness and desire, to POUR OUT of His boundless supply, His unlimited power, His unqualified and lavish goodness, joy, exuberance, and love.

> The heavens declare the glory of God; and the firmament shows His handiwork. Day unto day utters speech, and night to night reveals knowledge. There is no speech nor language where their voice is not heard. Their line [sound] has gone out through all the earth and their words to the end of the world. Psa. 19:1-4a NKJV

Throughout scripture, as well as the earth in which we live, the character of God is revealed in an unmeasured, unprecedented flow of the giving of life. God is the giver of all good and perfect gifts, and He is the giver of life. We see an example of His uncalculated pouring out as He opens the windows of heaven and pours out blessings far beyond the capacity to receive (Mal. 3:10). Our God can do exceedingly, abundantly, above all that we can ask or think. As we come to know Him, we realize that God does not HAVE love, He IS love. He does not HAVE light, He IS light. And so, He does not simply GIVE, He IS giving. And His giving is the constant out-flowing, freely pouring essence of all that He is. Through the windows of heaven, He pours a different quality of transforming life from another realm.

GOD POURS: THE RAIN OF GOD

The first evidence of that thundering opening of the windows of heaven came close after that which we know as "the beginning." There had been an ending of what was begun, and a new beginning.

> In the six hundredth year of Noah's life, in the second month, the seventeenth day of the month, on that day all the fountains of the great deep were broken up, and the windows of heaven were

opened. And the rain was on the earth forty days and forty nights. Gen. 7:11-12

It is interesting to note that the great flood, whereby the Lord God brought judgment upon the earth, lifted the righteous high above all destruction and death. The rains were an unsurpassed outpouring. God opened the windows of heaven and loosed the fountains of the deep that He might pour out upon the earth waters which consumed every living manifestation of death and rebellion. Though the floodwaters destroyed, the fact that they destroyed a creation gone haywire in rebellion meant that to the righteous, they were the life-giving rains which provided newness of life. And so it is in many of life's occurrences, which our Heavenly Father allows. At first it seems to bring only devastation, in Him, all things work together for good.

In Biblical times in Palestine, rainfall was a vital ingredient to the survival of man. Timing, quantity, and distribution of rainfall was uncertain, and great faith was displayed by those who persistently credited and believed God to send the rain. The climate in that part of the world divides the year into a rainy and a dry season. Toward the end of October heavy rains begin, and are known as the early or former rains. The Hebrew word for former means "pourer." These rains pour intermittently, tapering off gradually through February. The latter rains refer to the heavy showers of March and April, coming before the harvest and the long summer drought.

The early rains soften the cracked earth for the plow, but the most vital and important rains are the latter or spring rains, awakening the growing creation into harvest. They quicken life already flourishing, and push it on. The latter rain is received more readily by the earth, which is not the cracked, hard and enduring earth of summer drought, but the plowed and aerated, soft and chastened earth of the fruitful garden. Just as steam rises in fragrant gardens following a warm spring rain, so the cloud of great glory is appearing upon the horizon. "In the light of the king's countenance is life; and his favor is as a cloud of the latter rain" (Pro. 16:15, KJV). The Spring Season is here and harvest is nigh.

For as the rain and the snow come down from heaven, and do not return there without watering the earth, and making it bear and sprout, and furnishing seed to the sower and bread to the eater; so shall My word be which goes forth from My mouth; it shall not return to Me empty, without accomplishing what I desire, and without succeeding in the matter for which I sent it. Isa.55:10-11

What a precious promise this is! To know that the Word of God which established the earth and every living thing still falls into our living earth, the new earth, the Body of Christ, and will not die there, but will accomplish the purposes of the Most High God. He perfects those things which concern us, and in a constant all-encompassing flow of divine life. His Word pours through earthen vessels in just as uncompromisingly powerful a flow as the thunder of rain in those longed-for latter rains before Harvest. "For He whom God has sent speaks the words of God; for He gives the Spirit without measure" (John 3:34).

In Jesus dwells the fullness of the Godhead bodily (Col. 2:9). There was no limit to the measure of God in which He operated. But what is God's measure to man? We know that there has been given to every man the measure of faith (Rom. 12:3). Would God give His Spirit in unlimited measure to Jesus and then give only limited measure to man? May it never be! For it is written,

And He Himself gave some to be apostles, some prophets, some evangelists, and some pastors and teachers for the equipping of the saints for the work of ministry, for the edifying of the body of Christ, TILL WE ALL COME to the unity of the faith and of the knowledge of the Son of God, to a perfect man, TO THE MEASURE OF THE STATURE OF THE FULLNESS OF CHRIST. Eph. 4:11-13 NKJV

When a seed is planted, great care is taken to place it in a hole or container that is the right size. But in no way does the size of the seed or the place made for it limit the capacity of the plant to reach the height of maturity ordained for it. The container simply continues to enlarge to accommodate the growth. The tiny mustard seed bursts out of the earth into another realm, reaching to the skies in stately majesty. And so we, given a measure of faith, continue to water, weed, and fertilize, until from glory to glory we come to the measure of the stature of the fullness of Christ—in whom there is no limitation.

The Greek word for "fullness" in Eph. 4:13 is "pleroma," meaning "full number, full complement, full measure, plenitude, that which has been completed. The word describes a ship with a full cargo and crew, and a town with no empty houses. Pleroma strongly emphasizes fullness and completion" (The Spirit-Filled Life Bible, Word Wealth, page 1792). We are complete in Him! In Him, we experience the power of the fullness of eternity, the force of the river whose streams make glad the city of God.

Today God's principle of pouring out is becoming more and more apparent as His Body, the Body of Christ, learns to give. Many sermons have been taught and expounded upon over the last decades concerning the principle of giving in God's Word. Seed-faith. Sowing a seed into the need or the ministry of someone else. We have heard much about giving to get, or giving in order to receive blessing.

But as we apply ourselves to learn the principle of God's giving, we see that there is no thought of giving that there might be a return. It is simply an unmeasured, extraordinary pouring out, pouring out, pouring out. It is GOD'S principle of pouring out. In this pouring out He establishes a life-flow. He pours out and the earth answers by pouring back to Him, and as the earth answers by pouring back to Him, He pours out. Rain is loosed upon the earth. Then mist rises from the ground and seeds the clouds with moisture, whereby subsequent rain is released upon the obedient earth in glad showers. The cycle of life begins all over again. This graphically illustrates the principle of God's nature as He pours out.

And it will come about after this that I will pour out My Spirit on all mankind; and your sons and daughters will prophesy, your old men will dream dreams, your young men will see visions. And even on the male and female servants I will pour out My Spirit in those days. Joel 2:28-29

The pouring out of His Spirit upon His earth is immediately followed by His people pouring out of His Spirit in prophecy, dreams, and visions. The filled vessel is immediately pouring out gladly that precious supply, knowing that the Source is never dry. Man learns His principle of measure: there is none. Man carefully measures after assiduously assessing the supply. Man therefore in measured pouring has a measured supply and consequently a measured return. But no rain equals no growth and no growth equals stagnation and eventually death. So when man carefully measures, he is choosing a way which seems right to him, but the end thereof is death (Prov. 14:12).

"For in the way you judge, you will be judged; and by your standard of measure, it will be measured to you" (Matt. 7:2). Calculated measure contains an element of holding back. It is an attitude which calculates and decides "there is x amount in supply, x amount needed, and x amount allotted to fill that need, taking into account the price in pouring out." In essence it is a stingy spirit, taking more thought for self, in lack of faith, than acknowledging and operating in the flow of God's unprecedented, pouring out love.

As Jesus came upon the earth, a visible manifestation of all that God is, He poured out His life, His power, His Spirit, His character, His nature, and all the fullness of God. He did so without measure into the seed, into the earth which God had given Him (John 17:2,8,22), thus God continuing to pour out through His Son. The Spirit of Christ Jesus cried out in David's messianic prophecy, "I am poured out like water" (Psa. 22:14). King David was a forerunner of that second Adam Who thirsted upon the cross. While fleeing for his life into the caves and the rocks and the hills, David became very thirsty (2 Sam. 23:15). And so his mighty men went to draw, at the risk of their lives, from the wells of Bethlehem that he might have water. But David poured out this offering upon the ground; he poured out this precious substance brought at such a price upon the earth as an offering to the Lord. He exemplified the pouring nature of God by pouring back to Him what was given.

David didn't hold back enough to assuage his thirst and then empty the rest on the ground. He didn't tithe the water. He poured it out unreservedly before the Lord of Glory. Even so Jesus poured out His life upon and into the earth as an offering to His Father. He has bought us that we might pour out into the earth our lives and the preciousness of all of our substance, even as Jesus our big brother poured out, that life might come. This is the reciprocity of God.

When God gave His Son, it pleased Him to bruise Him, because Jesus justified many, pouring out His soul unto death (Isa. 53:10-12). There was no withholding in the outpouring of life to save many lives. There is no measure in God's mercy. "Thy lovingkindness, O Lord, extends to the heavens, Thy faithfulness reaches to the skies" (Psa. 36:5). There is no measure in the love of God, so majestically described in the old hymn,

O the deep, deep love of Jesus,
Vast unmeasured, boundless, free!
Rolling as a mighty ocean
In its fullness over me!
Underneath me, all around me
Is the current of Thy love
Leading onward, leading homeward
To Thy glorious rest above!

"Then shall we know, if we follow on to know the Lord: His going forth is prepared as the morning; and He shall come unto us as the rain, as the latter and former rain unto the earth" (Hos. 6:3, KJV). The torrential floods of the latter rains have scarcely begun to thunder upon our earth. There is coming such a flood of His grace, His love, and His manifested power, that surely all the fountains of the deep will be loosed, and the windows of heaven opened. We will never come to the end of our God, and His infinite love and yearning, brooding and hovering over this, His garden and His beloved.

HE POURS: THE WELLS OF GOD

As the rains fell upon parched and thirsty earth, man in times past learned to store and even milk the earth of its precious substance. We, the new earth, are the same. Natural and spiritual wells.

Whosoever drinks of the water that I shall give him shall never thirst; but the water that I shall give him shall be in him a well of water springing up into everlasting life. John 4:14 NKJV

The woman at the well had been drawing water for a long time. She was dependent, as were all others in the village, upon the fresh, cool substance. It was foreign and new to her that there could be other water, "living" water, freely given and that furthermore, she herself might give— just as she had served the stranger in her midst. In serving the Word incarnate, she learned that she could have the essence of this mystery of life somehow inside herself, to freely serve to others.

When I received the Baptism of the Holy Spirit and began to eat of the living bread in a new, fresh realm, the awe and joy of the water of the Word of God never palled. It never fell flat, or hung silent on the air. It had life and power that never failed to thrill and excite. Many of us will return to our first love in the days ahead, and find a second honeymoon with the Word of God. "Therefore with joy shall ye draw water out of the wells of salvation" (Isa. 12:3). The water of the Word out of these precious wells will serve that very life, joy and power to others wherever we go.

Sadly enough, the Body of Christ sometimes seems ignorant of the very substance which they carry with them everywhere. Even when the dryness of the wilderness around cries out in death throes, even when surrounded by difficult circumstances, we, the Body of Christ, hold within us the water of life so freely given. Then Israel sang this song, Spring up, O well; sing ye unto it (Num. 21:17). Like the woman at the well, let us joyfully embrace the truth that there is water which the world knows not of, and we, the keeper of the wells, hold the keys of life.

There are two kinds of wells: the slow and arduous let-down-the-bucket kind, and the free-flowing, everlasting artesian kind. The wells of salvation flow freely, generated by the supernatural power of God, and are not dependent upon human strength and zeal. Entering into God's rest means allowing the bubbling up, the springing up of that eternal, joyful flow. We cease from our own labors and trade them in for that priceless and infinite supply. "Heal the sick, raise the dead, cleanse the lepers, cast out demons; freely you received, freely give" (Matt. 10:8). As we command the opening of the windows of heaven within, we will activate the powerful flow of the life of God meant to flood the earth with His glory.

HE POURS: THE RIVERS OF GOD

Another mighty evidence of the great outpourings of the heavens are the rivers which run swiftly down the mountains, into the valleys, across the plains and fields and on to the sea. "And a river went out of Eden to water the garden" (Gen.2:10). "And he showed me A PURE RIVER OF WATER OF LIFE, clear as crystal, proceeding out of the throne of God and of the Lamb" (Rev. 22:1).

> How precious is Your lovingkindness, O God! Therefore the children of men put their trust under the shadow of Your wings. They are abundantly satisfied with the fullness of Your house, And You give them drink from the river of Your pleasures. For with You is the fountain of life; In Your light we see light.
> Psa. 36:7-9 NKJV

The river of God is of course the flowing current of Himself, the Living Word, Jesus being the first born of many brethren and the great reservoir of this divine water of life. "There is a river whose streams make glad the city of God, the holy dwelling places of the Most High" (Psa. 46:4). The joy and delight released by the river of God is the strength of His people. Our God inhabits the praises of His people, and as we release our praises to Him, the river of God is again a living, flowing stream, teeming with the resurrection power of life.

"Blessed are they who know the joyful sound" (Psa. 89:15). Mechanics will tell you that they can ascertain the problem in a vehicle by the sound of the engine. When there are problems in a church or in an individual life, one can always tell by the sounds of limited praise. The river is dammed up! But blessed ("happy, prosperous, well") are they who know and who participate in and who make a joyful sound! When we come joyously praising before the Lord with thankful hearts, regardless of what the circumstances are, we take up the shield of faith whereby we quench the fiery darts of the wicked one who wants to steal our joy and stop the flow of the river of God.

Over a period of many years, the Lord has trained me to practice His Presence, because I carry it with me at all times—all I need do is LET HIM OUT! In any service anywhere in the world, I am in His Presence. It doesn't depend upon the musicians, it doesn't depend on the pastor or the leadership, and it doesn't depend on the people. It depends on me. If I walk into a service thirsty, I loose the living waters that are within me, and immediately I am inundated with the Presence of the Lord because His Presence is within me. He is in me, and I am in Him; my soul thirsts for Him (Psa. 63:1).

> Ho! Everyone who thirsts, come to the waters; and you who have no money, come, buy and eat. Yes, come, buy wine and milk without money and without price. Isa 55:1 NKJV

The Holy Spirit is a living stream of this water flowing through the Body of Christ, released in torrents by the praises of God's people, who are often dry and parched from the wilderness of the world. The forces of the world, the flesh, and the devil do all that they can to stop the flow of worship. The devil hates the praises of God's people. For this reason, controversy is always spawned and perpetrated in, around, or about worship and the ministers who encourage and lead it. The priesthood of the believer, as he ministers to the living God, is a constant source of irritation, fear, and threat to the enemy.

Just as natural water is made of two natural elements, hydrogen and oxygen, so the water of life is also made of two: the Spirit and the Word. "It is the Spirit who gives life; the flesh profits nothing. The words that I speak to you are spirit, and they are life" (John 6:63-64 NKJV). Both these powerful and explosive elements are necessary for life. Either the Spirit or the Word alone could bring imbalance, fanaticism or legalism. But together, they produce that living stream which satisfies thirst in a dry land. We are a kingdom of priests, a living temple, and a throne for the King of all Kings.

> And he showed me a pure river of water of life, clear as crystal, PROCEEDING OUT OF THE THRONE OF GOD AND OF THE LAMB. Rev. 22:1

The River of God is proceeding, pouring through us. The throne, the resting place of God is within us, Mount Zion, the City of God, the Body of Christ (the Lamb). A river is a channeled concentrated current or stream of life flowing within banks. Nothing flows out which has not first flowed in. As He pours His Presence, His Word, His joy, His life, through us in that living stream, we continue the life-flow by pouring it back to Him. We can only minister out of the overflow of our own abundance. The stream of the Life of God is contained within the "banks" of our earthen vessel. So the Rivers of Life flow out of us, the Temple of the Holy Spirit, the New Jerusalem, and the dwelling place of God—out of OUR BELLY (John 7:37-39, KJV).

In this last day, as we enter the season of the last great feast, Jesus' Body is crying out to a lost and dying world even as Jesus did, "If any man thirst, come and drink of the waters of life!" Surely out of our belly shall flow rivers of living water (John 7:38)! The Greek word for "flow" means "to pour forth, to utter, speak, or say." The word for "belly" means the innermost part of a man. In other words, we are not talking about the brain! A popular chorus of long ago sings "Heaven is in My Heart." Out of the heaven of our heart, our innermost being, our belly, pours forth rivers of water which will never run dry.

OPEN THE GATES!

Even as the Lord of Glory opens the floodgates of Heaven, so we have gates which unleash the power of the rivers of living water. He says I will call your walls salvation, and your gates praise (Isa. 60:18). Gates in ancient times were, with the walls of the city, both a protection and a defense. Gates were always shut and locked at nightfall, and were the most vulnerable part of the city. An important meeting place, they provided a common ground where the elders of the city met and counseled together, and even sat in judgment (Isa. 28:6). The importance of the city gate was an undisputed fact.

But the Lord prophesied to His people that a day would come when physical protection and defense would be unnecessary, and that the physical fortresses would become obsolete as the Spirit of the Lord took their place.

The raging violence and emotional turmoil within our "city" will cease; the endless war between our members will be replaced by the praises of our God. Unlike the ancient city at nightfall, when trials and darkness seem to fall in our lives, we will open wide the gates of praise—not close the Lord out! Lift up your heads, O gates, and be lifted up, O ancient doors, that the King of glory may come in (Psa. 24:7)!

In King David's time, the gates of the city were hung from the top on great hinges, so that they were lifted to open and lowered to close. The King of Glory waits to enter His temple. Have we lowered the gates against Him? The thundering hosts of Heaven accompany Him as He travels victoriously through time and space, hurling thunderbolts and lightning flashes in abundance. That we in our frail houses of straw and earth would dare to "close" anything against Him exposes our ignorant, obtuse--and determined! —path to destruction. But when we open the gates of praise and the gates of righteousness (Psa. 118:19), the King of Glory comes in and goes out. He pours Himself in, and we pour Him out and all are changed in His glory.

We find in the New Jerusalem, that holy city adorned as a bride for her husband, that the gates are never shut (Rev. 21:25). Within us are the floodgates of the waters of Life. Just as the gates of the New Jerusalem are never shut, so our gates are always open, allowing the rivers of the Most High to flow out unhindered and unmeasured.

Jesus is the gate. "I am the gate; whoever enters through Me will be saved. He will come in and go out, and find pasture" (John 10:9, NIV). The Shepherd is the gate. He is the water. He is the joy. He is the crown. And as He is, so are we in this world (1 John 4:7). As we pour out of the windows of heaven within, flooding our earth with thundering treasure, all around us the water level will begin to rise.

The Lord portrayed graphically the rising of the waters when His hand came upon the prophet Ezekiel, taking him up in the visions of God to a high mountain. There the Lord revealed to him a new temple and a new order of worship. In the temple, Ezekiel saw what John saw in a later vision: water flowing from the threshold of the temple, water pouring from the throne of God (Eze. 47:1, Rev. 22:1). As the water was measured, it began to rise, first to the ankles, then to the knees, to the waist, and finally, a river that he could not cross, deep waters to swim in.

We have seen those waters of the Spirit rise throughout history as the Body of Christ experienced each restoration and move of the Holy Spirit. The Lord is calling to His people: "My voice, My Presence, My power, My healing river, is stored like treasure, in earthen vessels. My river of many waters is within you." The voice of the Lord is like the sound of many waters.

> And behold, the glory of the God of Israel was coming from the way of the east. And His voice was like the sound of many waters; and the earth shone with His glory. Eze. 43:2

The many waters are the streams flowing from the corporate, many-membered Son, the Body of Christ. And this is the plan fulfilled: that all the earth shall be filled with the glory of the Lord as the waters cover the sea (Num. 14:21). The river of God freely flowing out of its earthen banks will bring glory, healing and life to all the earth, seeding it unto harvest.

RICH BUILDING MATERIALS ALONG THE RIVERS

As we study the river in Eden, we see that the river that was one became four after leaving Eden (Gen. 2:10). Four is the symbolic number of earth, i.e., four seasons, four winds, four corners. Along these rivers were precious stones and gold, speaking of the glory and nature of God. The majesty and splendor of God was always reflected in His dwelling places in gold and silver, in precious stones and colors of strong hues. God's foreshadowing of the ultimate resting place of His Spirit was displayed in great detail in Moses' Tabernacle.

"The Tabernacle in the wilderness, constructed to God's specific detailed instructions, was resplendent with gold and silver, costly jewels, and vivid colors; the Ark of His Presence was inlaid of hammered gold. The priests were arrayed in garments of great and intricate beauty. It was there that the Lord met with Moses, between the wings of the cherubim." (Quoted from the author's book, "Celebration," page 17) (See Ex. 25:3-4; Ex. 25:7-8).

Now His temple is built of living stones, even more beautiful, alive and living with His beauty and His power (1 Pet. 2:4-5). Wherever the River flows, materials will be found for the completion of the Temple. "And the Lord their God will save them in that day as the flock of His people; for they are as the stones of a crown, sparkling in His land" (Zech. 9:16). The Lord God is completing and perfecting all that concerns us as His living temple, that dwelling place of great splendor, radiant with the Father's glory. The entire holy city through which this river flows is constructed with all manner of splendorous and diaphanous jewels singing a symphony of the beauty of the Lamb.

> And I saw no temple therein: for the Lord God Almighty and the
> Lamb are the temple of it. Rev. 21:18-22

Everywhere in the New Jerusalem, the Holy City, we see shouts and trumpet fanfares of the splendor of life. The City is inlaid with precious stones and golden streets, and the sparkling river of the waters of resurrection life healing everything it touches. But also along the river we find the re-appearance of the Tree of Life. The Tree of Life was rejected by Adam in Eden, and reappeared as Jesus the Bridegroom, giving man another chance to be complete. As He is the first-born, we become like Him, trees of righteousness, bearing leaves for the healing of the nations, sparkling and shining as the stones of a crown.

The four rivers out of Eden become one tumultuous River of Life in the New Jerusalem, signifying that the new creation, the Body and Bride of Christ have united, becoming one with another and with Him, the restored Eden, the Garden of the Lord. God pours forth waters of life in unmeasured supply through the Bride, the Body of Christ, to water the thirsty earth, seeded with the Word, to bring forth an Eternal Harvest and a radiant, Glorious Garden.

VIII

THE SUN AND LIGHT

His glory covered the heavens, and the earth was full of His praise.
And His brightness was like the sunlight; rays streamed from His
hand; and there in the sun-like splendor was the hiding place of
His power. Hab.3:3a-4 AMP

*Central thought: The greatness and living warmth of the essence of God's
eternal Light, Ever Increasing upon the earth, is combining with abundant
Living Waters to bring forth massive, unprecedented Harvest and an
opulent, effusive, expansive, ever-increasing Garden shining with the Light
and Glory of the King.*

GOD MADE THE SUN TO RULE BY DAY (PSA. 136:8).

The light of the sun is necessary for all life. In Eden, even as it is today,
there was light called day, and darkness called night. In the world of nature,
a riotous birdsong heralds the coming light of day, and with the rising of
the sun, all nature goes about busily mating, building homes, and feeding
their young. Activity slows with the waning light. Plants fold up their leaves
in the darkness, and much of nature sleeps through the quiet evening
shadows, while predators hide in the darkness, choosing obscurity as a veil
to stalk unsuspecting prey.

Hungry for light, plants seek it greedily, their growth directly affected
by the amount of light received. Vegetation left too long in the dark will

wilt and eventually die. In forests thick enough to block out sunlight overhead, plant growth on the ground is limited to the most hardy and dark-loving. Fields are planted in full sun, allowing maturing crops unlimited access to the life-giving light. Most flower-bearing plants only flourish in sunlight, unfurling their colorful petals to greet the sun with joy.

As a single young adult making my way in the concrete jungle of a large inner city, I longed for growing green things to soften and cheer my small dark apartment. And so each spring, renewed by the happy growth outside, I went to nurseries and bought flourishing plants. Summer marked their gradual decline. Fall indicated that they were sick, sick. By winter, I sadly threw away pots of dead brown unrecognizables. There simply was not enough light in my little corner of the world to foster growth. But each spring—you guessed it—back to the nursery!

All creation comes alive in the light. Most of us have experienced walking in gardens or parks or arboretums on a cloudy day, when suddenly shafts of sunlight peek out and sift through the trees. Even humdrum plants become exotic and beautiful with illumination. As sunlight shines through leaves and petals, delicate veins and intricate patterns suddenly become visible. Subtle differences in colors and hues intensify, and joy begins to sing through the air like the hum of katydids and the cries of wild living creatures.

In the centuries of the flowering of what we now call the great Masters of oil painting such as Rembrandt, one of the secrets of greatness lay in the treatment of dark and light. The sharp pitting of great light against deep darkness produced startling, jewel-like qualities imitated for centuries and still emulated and praised today. Chiaroscuro: light vs darkness.

For example, place a flower or plant in a dark room next to a window, and the plant will lean and yearn toward the light to the extent that it will grow that way permanently if left in that position. This process is known as phototropism. Even the tribe of Judah, in the wilderness, pitched camp toward the east, or the sunrise (Num. 2:3). All creation, in its darkness, yearns toward the rising of the sun of righteousness with healing in His wings.

The sun rules by day. It decides how hot or how cold the atmosphere will be; whether there will be snow or rain; whether ships will sail or children will play. The presence of the sun determines whether its subjects freeze or burn. This makes misusing the attributes of the sun dangerous to healthy life. The sun is the center of its universe, and every created thing revolves around it. The sun can be our best friend and our worst enemy, but no matter how we feel about it, we will all agree that we cannot live without it.

The psalmist says that God the Father is the sun and shield of our lives. He is both the heat and the shade from the heat. He is the center around which our universe revolves, and He is the sun Who rules our day. He rises with us in the morning and abides with us all the day. When clouds hide His face from our view, He is still present everywhere, always shining, steadily abiding in the all-encompassing Presence of Himself as the great I AM.

God the Father is the source and direct cause of all life and growth. The absence of His Presence is the ice of death, and His omnipresence is a consuming fire. Mis-using His power is like playing carelessly with atomic power. Falling into the hands of the living God is a frightening, glorious experience of startling unadulterated undiluted raw LIGHT. It sears and burns away all not created to carry its flame. It kindles to life all that carries and bears its own nature. The Presence of the Lord is the experience of the natural sun magnified as far as the heavens are above the earth.

The Lord of Hosts is a goad which painfully spurs us on toward His goal. He is a caress carrying both a witness and a warning: a witness of a love beyond the natural ability to comprehend and a warning of the coldness of death without Him. He is a sword which divides and hews out cancerous growth, accomplishing surgery and healing at the same time.

The Lord God is a shining which causes the stretching of growth, the change necessitated by it, and the joy which results from it. The shining of His Presence forces hope from frozen earth, shouts of life from the iciness of the grave, and abiding peace from the trust of His rising. The Lord God calls us from comfort, beguiles us from ease, and roots us up out of familiar lying places. The warmth of His light compels us to throw off grave clothes and run from the coffins of desire. It exposes the hidden ashes of past fires and blows upon banked coals content to sit and simmer.

The stirring of our sun and shield engenders respect for His strategies of war and soothes nerves frozen into inactivity by jangling fears and helpless tears. The whirlwind of His fire sweeps dust clouds of His glory before Him, and shakes the mountains into terror before the splendor of His majesty.

THE SUN OF RIGHTEOUSNESS RISES

Jesus, the Light of the world and the Daystar, is the exact representation and extension of all that God the Father is. He is the bright and morning star, rising in the darkness of the night sky with the sure and pure shining of hope eternal. "He is the sole expression of the glory of God—the Light-being, the out-raying of the divine—and He is the perfect imprint and very image of [God's] nature, upholding and maintaining and guiding and propelling the universe by His mighty word of power" (Heb. 1:3a, AMP).

Even as the Lord God made the sun to rule by day and the moon to rule by night, so across the ages we see the prevailing principle of the sun and light. In the beginning, God said, "Let there be light!" and the revelation of light filled the earth. God Himself, Who IS light, revealed light to all of His creation. When man fell in the Garden of Eden, he chose to go away from the light, and as the Lord's plan of redemption unfolded, man lived by the light of the moon for many centuries. The lesser light ruled during the darkness of the ages while man worked out his redemption in fear and trembling.

God's desire is to have, for all eternity, a companion of like nature and ability. "By this, love is perfected with us, that we may have confidence in the Day of Judgment; because as He is, so also are we in this world" (1 John 4:17). God isn't looking for robots to do His bidding; He isn't a giant taskmaster in the sky who needs helpers. The Lord of Hosts has planned a kingdom of priests, sprung from His own Seed, made of His substance, and cleaving only to Him for all eternity.

In Sunday school as a child we were taught a little song, "Jesus Wants Me for a Sunbeam!" I never understood the profound significance of those simple words. God, the great Sun Who rules our day, desires children of His own nature, beams and shafts and rockets of that same vibrant sunlight holding the worlds together. The plan of God, unfolded at great cost and revealed in its fullness with infinite patience, put a man at the helm of the vast ship of the ages. Adam was created in the image and likeness of God (Gen. 1:26-27).

The Hebrew word translated "image," is "tselem," which means "shade, phantom, resemblance": literally, a shadow. In fact, the actual word shadow comes from the root of the word image. At the time of his creation, Adam was a shadow of the substance, a shade in the shape of the sun. His ultimate destiny was to eat of the Tree of Life in the midst of the garden and become complete. His desire for knowledge rather than life led to the separation of the shadow from the substance, leaving him to wander through the ages in his formless and empty state. "When Adam had lived one hundred and thirty years, he became the father of a son IN HIS OWN LIKENESS, according to HIS IMAGE, and named him Seth" ("substitute") (Gen.5:3). Adam substituted the image of God for the image of a shadow lost from its moorings.

God's infinite wisdom and mercy woven together formed a net of redemption by which Jesus, the Tree of Life, returned to provide meat and drink that man might taste and see that the Lord is good (John 6:56). The Son of God, perfect and sinless and exactly like His Father became the sacrificial lamb, and the Light given to gather others. In partaking of the offering so generously provided, the shadow became one with the substance as was planned in the heart of the Father since before the beginning. "Therefore let no one act as your judge in regard to food or drink or in respect to a festival or a new moon or a Sabbath day—things which are a mere shadow of what is to come; but the substance belongs to Christ" (Col. 2:16-17).

Jesus came, the substance at last, that He might provide the womb of the morning for all creation. *"For there is coming the matrix."* (From the Preface of this book.) The word "matrix" means "something within which something else originates or develops," and "material in which something is enclosed or embedded for protection or study." It is the original, providing not only the prototype, but the mold for others. He, and we in Him, are not the shadow but the substance.

The old covenant was the light of the moon ruling by night. But the old was fulfilled in the new. With the rising of the Daystar, Jesus, the Light of the world, the Son of righteousness, the old was fulfilled in the new. Darkness was dispersed by the light and a new covenant was instituted.

> And so we have the prophetic word made more sure, to which you
> do well to pay attention as to a lamp shining in a dark place, until
> the day dawns and the morning star arises in your hearts.
> 2 Pet. 1:19

We are complete in Him. As His light dawns in our hearts and He rises to take His place as King in our lives, WE are the light of the world, the called out ones, the overcomers who rule the day with Him. The higher the sun rises in the midst of the day, the smaller and smaller the shadow, until fullness comes and the shadows flee away completely. "But the path of the righteous is like the light of dawn, that shines brighter and brighter until the full day" (Prov. 4:18). The shadow and the substance become one, as the shadow is changed from glory to glory into maturity and union. Night is superseded by day as the Daystar rises brighter and brighter until the full day and there is no darkness to be found in the light of His countenance.

WINDOW OF HOPE

Through the window a new dawn lights the horizon. A new day is on the threshold. And seers peering into the realm of God's mighty Spirit see a vast Light rising in the darkness of this present age. Prophets everywhere are calling mankind to the window to see history in the making. Man, on his way to the window, wonders if his ship is finally coming in. Just like the disciples who looked for an earthly kingdom and a reigning king, man is looking for some kind of "reward" for his labors.

There are many types of payment, many types of reward and many types of currency. Man is always looking for his reward and payment, constantly demanding to know what the currency is, or the medium of exchange. If I do this, what will I get, and if I do that what will be given to me? Man is always looking for a return on the act of his will and on the result of his labors. He doesn't want to work for nothing. He doesn't want to put forth effort without the assurance of knowing that immediately something will come back. And so he works with his eye on the payment; he labors with his attention on the reward.

He is trapped in the film of a time/space dimension, always looking from one frame to the next, in order to have the courage to proceed from one place into the next. But God is taking the foot of man and causing it to step upon the waters of eternity: out of one realm into another. And the payment of his labors in this time/space dimension is a payment in hope. For his reward of hope opens his eyes at last to see his release from this prison of time and this bondage of doing in order to get, walking ahead in exchange for something. The payment for obedience to the King of Kings is the hope of a better realm. It is the hope of a better life, the hope of a greater understanding, the hope of a broader expectation, the hope of a deeper encouragement, the hope of a keener joy, the hope of expansive revelation and the hope of eternal existence.

Hope is a window through which man can see God's plan. It is like the window on a spaceship. Inside the spaceship, except for weightlessness, the astronaut is surrounded by the things of his own world. But through the window of the spaceship lies an expanse of uncharted territory, foreign experience, and different air. The astronaut is well content to stay within the confines of his own understanding, with his instruments, calculations, measurements and his spacesuit.

But the Lord desires that man leap through the window of hope into that other place where he is not bound by the cords of the adversities of life nor chained to the doors of anxiety. He is not lashed to the post of diligence; the manacles upon his ankles don't hobble him to the walls of anger. But the hymns and songs and praises of deliverance have set the captives free, that man may fly from the evidences of his terror out of the dungeons of despair, through the window of hope, leaving behind familiar instruments of bondage.

So many choose to remain shackled by familiarity. Others would rather submit to the tortures of the known than to leap through the door of hope into the unknown joys and delights of another realm, another time, another space, another experience: prisoners of hope. No longer prisoners of desire in a realm of legalism and knowledge, but prisoners of hope, having left the old behind, content to walk according to the life of the spirit. The dawn or the breaking of the day is the promise, the hope, of the fullness of the day. The dawning of a new day is upon the horizon.

> Because of the tender mercy of our God, with which the Sunrise from on high shall visit us, to shine upon those who sit in darkness and the shadow of death, to guide our feet into the way of peace. Luke 1:78-79

Man will walk by the light of the sun and no longer strive in the dimness and shadows of the moon. For though the moon was a blessing in the darkness, in the light of the sun there will be no need for the moon, one having moved from the lesser light to the greater light. Then one has moved from the work/reward system through the door of hope into the cycles of life and become whirlwinds and fireballs of the energy of God, rolling through eternity. Then man roars through uncharted space with no thought of mileage or effort or labor or payment or reward, but is content in the privilege of going, content to generate, to operate, content to burst forth with life, content to explode with the regenerative miraculous and joyous nature of Him Who is the wind and the rain and the thunder and the song. In that day, man has moved into the realm where there is no darkness, and where he has become one with the vast ball of brilliance around which the universe lives and moves and has its being.

THE SUN STOOD STILL

> Then Joshua spoke to the Lord in the day when the Lord delivered up the Amorites before the children of Israel, and he said in the sight of Israel: "Sun, stand still over Gibeon; and Moon, in the valley of Ajalon. So the sun stood still, and the moon stopped, till the people had revenge upon their enemies…So the sun stood still in the midst of heaven, and did not hasten to go down for about a

whole day. And there was no day like that before it or after it, that the Lord heeded the voice of a man: for the Lord fought for Israel. Joshua 10:12-14 NKJV

What a day this was! God's messenger, His servant Joshua, spoke with the authority of His God TO His God. Notice that "Joshua spoke TO THE LORD," and said, "SUN." Joshua did not ask the Lord to cause the sun to stand still. He did not beg for favor. He did not plead for Israel. He simply spoke to the Lord through His creation with the authority to stop time for a space. Joshua used the dominion and authority over the entire universe that God gave to Adam in the beginning.

"Joshua" the savior of God's people was bringing the people in to possess the land, and in order to do that, war had to be waged. As the battle raged, Joshua saw that there was need in this unique time/space dimension that eternity invade mortality for a space and delay the darkness—a miraculous provision that those on the battlefield of life might finish their fight in the light of God's day.

God the Sun stood still in the heavens as the war raged, that enemies be dethroned and powers vanquished and the sons of God came to full realization of who indeed they really are. Many have wondered about God's timetable, moving close to bitterness as they conjecture about "delays" in the fulfillment of God's promises. Is God on vacation? Is He away from the phone? Has He had a lapse of memory? Are man's puny affairs beneath His notice and not worth His time?

But the great I Am Who neither slumbers nor sleeps, in His infinite patience and His unfailing mercy, has stilled His rising that man might grow to maturity in complete unity with the tempo of the culmination of the ages. Can a nation be born in a day? Were the worlds flung into space in not much more than that? But God has graciously ordained that man, who could be burned to smithereens in one blast of God's breath, have time to develop other-world muscles and nostrils that can breathe air in another realm.

God is allowing us to grow to His level. How many leaders today can learn from God's example as they bring the little ones alongside, training for reigning? Would that we partake of the patience of our everlasting

Father with those around us, as we nurture, feed and encourage the young in the Lord to venture out bravely. God allowed man to make his mistakes, over and over, through countless ages, as He prepared a Bride for His Son. Jesus prayed, "that they may be one as we are one" (John 17). What has happened with that prayer for unity?

Let us, as beams and shafts of that great Light, WAIT on the timing of the Lord—not only for ourselves, but also for one another. Let us allow the time needed for those that the Lord has given us to grow and develop, making and learning from their own mistakes, while we shine the umbrella and warmth of our anointing over them, covering all, loving all, and brooding over the young even as the Spirit of God did over the earth in that long ago beginning.

And the Sun stood still. Hallelujah!!!

PRINCIPLE OF EVER-INCREASING LIGHT

As the sons of God move into maturity and union with the great Fire of all life, they are being changed from glory to glory, into veritable fireballs of that same life, power and energy. The shinings of the great I Am will radiate and pulsate from the innermost being of man much like the transfiguration on the mountain when God allowed His eternal light to be perceived with the natural eyes of a mortal man, far ahead of the manifestation of the radiant ones of the kingdom. "And He was transfigured before them; and His face shone like the sun, and His garments became as white as light" (Matt.17:2).

> And the teachers and those who are wise shall shine like the brightness of the firmament; and those who turn many to righteousness—to uprightness and right standing with God shall give forth light like the stars forever and ever. Daniel 12:3 AMP

"But let those who love Him be like the sun when it comes out in full strength" (Judges 5:31b). Have you ever sat in a massive candle lighting service when all the lights are turned off and a single candle starts the process of the multiplication of light? Gradually, as hundreds of candles are lit, the room begins to shimmer and shine. Even as a cloud is made up of many particles to form one visible unified form, so God's cloud of Light and Glory is made up of many members: all parts of one Body, each individual light combining to make one large mass of brilliance. In these last days, as creation moves toward maturity, the light of the Lamb shines from His children, the Body of Christ, the spotless and jeweled Bride. The Light that came into the world has given birth to veritable powerhouses, lighthouses which beam into the darkness of this present age, passing the torch, carrying and multiplying the light until all the earth shines with His glory.

For even as one walks along the endless shores of the seas and waters of life, and the piercing call of a bird thrills the heart with its sweetness, the balm in soft winds caress the cheek and petals fall and fragrance rides along the avenues of the breath of God, so is the love of God waiting ever ready, ever joyful to reach the hungry heart. He is the initiator, the aggressor, the wooer. And man—man sometimes turns away, sorrowful or bitter or just empty—and sometimes he responds and opens that the King of Glory may come in. But always the Love and Light of God stands ever ready to fill the wasting wilderness that is man away from His God.

No sin is too heavy, no evil too thick to cover the Light, the true Light that came into the world to dispel the darkness. The people that walked in darkness HAVE SEEN, they have SEEN a great Light. Will they approach the Light or will they run away? Will they cover themselves in it, immersed, filled, sheathed, robed, and carried by the Light of the world? For this Light has a name and His name is Jesus. He walked upon this earth and He walks it still, alive and explosive in the hearts of men, dividing the Light from the darkness and calling it DAY.

The peoples of the world have had the Daystar arise in their hearts and have given Him place, His throne resting within. Indeed and they have arisen upon the face of the earth as a mighty constellation freshly created might march across the sky. They are blazing, singing, and dancing across the continents and seas, gathering momentum as they go, the power of the risen Christ growing greater and greater within them as they decrease and HE increases. With the clarion call of the Ancient of Days in their ears, they advance together, with single eye and undaunted heart, sparks of joy showering abroad as they go.

The glory of the Lamb will not suddenly beam down from some hidden and exalted place upon a needy and dark world, but it will stream in fullness from all those who bear His name. It will shine with increasing purity and strength, brighter and brighter until the full day. Just as Stephen's face shone as the angels, and Moses hid his radiance with a veil, so will the sons of God manifest the radiance of His glory. Life will be brighter than noonday and darkness will become like morning (Job 11:17, NIV).

NIGHT BOWS TO PERPETUAL LIGHT

Night has often seemed prolonged as the battles in darkness continued. But now, in this season of harvest and accelerated growth, the Son rises with more and more intensity, and night seasons lesson as the full day approaches. From this we see that in immaturity there are seasons of rest from the sun, and when full maturity comes, night is no longer necessary: the principle of Ever Increasing Light. Pressing into Him, we know more of God's Presence than we knew a year ago. There is a deeper infilling of His love and mercy and grace than there was five years ago. We are moving from glory to glory into more and more light, more illumination, and more enlightenment in the knowledge of Him.

"And we shall live in His sight" (Hosea 6:2). In the New Jerusalem there is no night, and the gates are never shut. In "that day," the third day, the seventh day, the FULL DAY, the day of full sun, there will be a Sabbath rest for the people of God, from their own labors. In this paradise, the new Eden, there will be no need of natural sun, for the Light of Life, the Lamb, will be the fullness of revelation and light: the realm of His fullness and perfection in which there is no darkness or shadow of turning. There will be no need of natural light, understanding, and intellect apart from the word of God and the mind of Christ. His light, His wisdom, His understanding will rule our hearts and minds with peace. And that same illumination will enlighten our eyes to behold Him. In the full day, we will all know as we are known. Now we see in part, but then face to face.

"For there is coming the matrix, and a pinnacle, a place that man has always desired to go, and tried to climb to, but could never reach. The pinnacle, out of the midst of the being of Mount Zion, will be reached in a day, in an hour, in a moment, literally in the twinkling of an eye." The Hebrew word for "sun" means "pinnacle." The coming of God's fullness is the coming of the sun in full strength—the pinnacle of warmth, light, life and joy.

The greatness and living warmth of the essence of God's eternal Light, Ever Increasing upon the earth, is combining with abundant Living Waters to bring forth massive, unprecedented Harvest and an opulent, effusive, expansive, ever-increasing Garden shining with the Light and Glory of the King.

IX

GROWTH

Central thought: God is raising up laborers, shafts of His great light, ever-increasing, ever-growing, ever-expanding, ever-multiplying their fruitfulness from this world into the next and into the next and into the next, an eternal ever-expanding ever-growing ever-glowing shining and radiant Garden of Great Glory.

THE PRINCIPLE OF GROWTH (INCREASE)

For all these things are taking place for your sake, so that the more grace (divine favor and spiritual blessing) extends to more and more people and multiplies through the many, the more thanksgiving may increase [and redound] to the glory of God…

For our light, momentary affliction (this slight distress of the passing hour) is ever more and more abundantly preparing and producing and achieving for us an everlasting weight of glory [beyond all measure, excessively surpassing all comparisons and all calculations, a vast and transcendent glory and blessedness never to cease!]. 2 Cor. 4:15,17 AMP

As God set the worlds into motion, His principle of multiplication was also set into motion. His dream was not to create a one-time permanent object which would remain the same as long as the worlds remain. But God's plan was to create a replica of Himself, to reproduce Himself. God's multiplication is not so much a principle of multiplying two times two, as it is a principle of the increase and the reproduction of the quintessence of the

Creator Himself. Not a multiplication of inanimate numbers, but reproduction of the life of God—an increase of His light, an expansion of His knowledge, and of His power and glory.

God's command to every beast of the field and to every created thing, as well as to the man that He created in His own image, was to "be fruitful and multiply" (Gen. 1:28). "Be fruitful" came first. And then the multiplication of that fruitfulness came second. God's plan was to put in motion a never-ending eternal progression of the development of a new nation. Adam was to be only the beginning.

MULTIPLICATION OF THE SEED: NOT THE DIRT

> As the host of heaven cannot be counted, and the sand of the sea cannot be measured, so I will multiply the descendants of David My servant and the Levites who minister to Me. Jer. 33:22

Note here that the people honored by God's choice of multiplication were the descendants of the man after God's own heart, and the ones dedicated to serving only the Lord. He took those with the essence of His heart and multiplied them more than any on the earth. God's principle of increase can be applied to many different circumstances, financial, material, physical, emotional and spiritual. But the principle remains the same. What is at the heart of God's principle of increase, as we see the good soil yield thirty, sixty, and a hundredfold (Matt. 13:8)?

So many books and studies have been made of giving and prosperity that further development is not necessary. Here we reopen the subject from a somewhat different angle. As we explore increase, multiplication, and giving according to God's plan, we notice that scripture states that good soil will yield, but with different levels of increase. Is the good soil referred to here, expectant soil, hopeful soil, innocent soil, righteous soil? Often we find society lamenting the loss of innocence in its world, all the while disparaging and criticizing all those who make a stand for what would be known as "righteousness."

Morality and right standing before God is immediately suspect, while innocence is touted and defiled at the same time. Various winds blow in ecclesiastical circles around giving and prosperity, while the world watches tongue-in-cheek for ministers to "fall from grace" and make mistakes appearing as a dark blot upon a white cloth. And all the while, the watchers, from their critical vantage point, are living those very mistakes as a way of life. The ones who would crucify the righteous for one mistake will defend the "innocent" to the death, as long as it is an innocent from their world. It is vitally important in this season of accelerated growth and increase that we understand with revelation GOD'S principle of increase, and the increase of WHAT.

GOD THE SEED IS RIGHTEOUS—NOT INNOCENT

Does the Lord look for soil that is innocent of any knowledge of good and evil, any knowledge or awareness of temptation? Or could He value soil that has seen (just like God in His omniscience sees) and yet has chosen God's path, after seeing both? After all, what is being multiplied is the seed—it may be any number and varieties of seed, but the life in all seed, all growth, is the Word of God, the essence of His Spirit. We know that God is righteous, not innocent (Psa. 145:17).

So what exactly IS innocence? Of course, we know that to be "innocent" of any wrongdoing means to be blameless or pure. Certainly, the Lord desires purity. But there is a state, or "age" of innocence, whereby the innocent is blameless because of ignorance and unawareness.

In the context that innocence is the absence, or ignorance, of the knowledge of evil, we become aware that the age of innocence can be a dangerous time. The age of innocence (as unawareness) is a time of inaction. It is a time of indecision. It is a time of inactivity. It is a time of unreality and fantasy. It is a time when the human soul has been untried and unproven. It is a time of immaturity and the possibility of ill-use. For the innocent are often used by those who have passed beyond the age of innocence. The innocent are venerated and applauded and even set up as demi-gods, but often used for less than innocent purposes.

But the righteous man can be of infinitely more value than those locked in the age of innocence. For innocence in its ignorance is blindness that shields man from traversing the wicked one's barriers in order that he might reach the other side of innocence to righteousness. The righteous man has learned to see that he once moved out of the age of innocence and became aware of an alternative to innocence, that being wickedness. But he chose to look beyond the wicked one and see in the face of Christ that God is good, and that none is good but God.

Consider the bubble babies who are kept inside a sterilized bubble, and can't be touched by human hands or anything outside their bubble, because their body has no immune system. Consequently, they are not allowed to partake of normal life and activity. They don't know what it is to be normal. They are encased in a bubble that is innocent of dirt and germs and virus and all of the things that attack a healthy human only to be repulsed by the healthy immune system. They are unable to function in an ordinary environment, or to interact with anyone outside their sphere.

This depicts the age of innocence, in its unawareness of any world but its own. Innocence is a bubble that protects and shields and keeps separate from normal life. But while innocence is a shield, it is also a wall that divides. And the worldly man, while residing in his evil territory, would look at the innocent on the one hand, and at the righteous on the other, and he would say that the innocent is to be venerated and lauded, because the innocent is untainted. (He bemoans his own loss of innocence and sees the sin in his own life, although he does nothing about it.) On the other hand, he mistakes and accuses the righteous of "self-righteousness." But he has no spirit to understand that the innocent is much less practical and useful to God than the righteous. For the righteous are valiant foes worthy of consideration, having tasted of the devil's bread and chosen living bread instead.

When you take the bubble baby out of his bubble, having healed his inner immune system, he can face the same germs that would once have killed him while he was in his bubble. He can laugh at their puny strength— and all that is within him will rise up to fight off the invader. So it is with the man who has come out of his innocence through the fields of temptation to walk into the kingdom of the Lord of Hosts and His righteousness. He walks in the Spirit at peace with who he is, not what he is judged or perceived to be.

ACCELERATED GROWTH

This season of harvest is a season of accelerated growth. In this season we will see the bubble babies, the innocent, catapulted over the fields of temptation and into the Kingdom at an accelerated rate. Testimonies will be shorter and shorter of the hell to heaven variety where innocence was deflowered and despoiled and then one walked through years of intimate acquaintance with the devil's workshop.

For the increase of the Lord will bring man at an accelerated and expansive rate, down the corridors of experience and into the sunlight of the knowledge of Christ. For the knowledge of good and evil which brought about Adam's separation from God, brought him into knowledge of false good, and knowledge of all of the devil's evil ways and acts. Man learned to visit satan in his workshop and watch him at play and work for his, man's, entertainment. Damaging and injuring the mind and the will and the emotions, the memories, the habits of the body, to such a degree, that years had to be spent in washing, cleansing and counseling and teaching about righteousness.

But the accelerated growth, of multiplication of the fruitfulness of God's creation, in this season of supernatural growth, many will shoot through that middle ground of acquaintance with the devil; many will be plucked from innocence, and taken directly into the righteousness of their King. They will be wise as serpents and harmless as doves. They will have no vengeance to overcome, no rancor, and no bitterness. They will not go through that terrible battle of mistaking man for their enemies in that middle kingdom ruled by the prince of the power of the air. They will grow into righteousness, recognizing and dealing effectively with the true enemy, the god of this world: the devil and all his henchmen.

The ever-increasing light of the glory of Christ upon the faces of the righteous will be the firstfruits, the first manifestation, of this season of growth and expansion. For the bubble babies, the innocent, will meet the Lord at an earlier age. They will become like Jesus, the sinless spotless Lamb Who knew no sin and yet was righteous because of His Father's righteousness; the Lamb Who walked with discernment, authority, and

155

justice in the midst of His purity. They will become like Enoch, who first walked here, and then walked there. They will walk out of innocence into righteousness without the pain and the sorrow and sighing of this world, without the veil of tears that must be rent by the crucifixion of flesh.

Like John the Baptist, who was filled with the Holy Spirit in his mother's womb, so the babies of the end-time harvest will be filled with the Spirit, growing in wisdom and power while in the womb. And as they make their entrance into this natural world, simultaneously they will make their entrance into the righteousness of their God, carrying their innocence with them. Carrying their purity with them, which will remain as they grow, carrying body, soul, and spirit untainted by the wiles of the devil and the thoughts of the wicked one.

Puberty will no longer be a foray into rebellion and a divided mind. It will no longer be a time of terrorizing parents and upsetting households. It will no longer be a time of total upheaval, when the mind and the body rebel against all authority. Perverse spirits will no longer rule the twelve, thirteen, and fourteen-year-olds of this world, for they will be transported into another realm, and walk in the spirit. They will walk in the fullness of God's nature.

Even as the young and protected in these last days are ushered into the realm of God's righteousness, so will those who have strayed into the kingdom of darkness, having become lost to light. For the Spirit of God will drag in the great harvest net and catch many unusual and unlikely fish. From all backgrounds, educations and cultures, from all levels of innocence, wariness, wiliness, and downright evil, God will make His call and receive overwhelming, unprecedented response. In this season of accelerated growth, we will see seed sown which will bear instant fruit. It will resemble more a transplanting of trees than the planting of a tiny seed.

Seed planting in the eternal realm in which God dwells bodily in all His fullness may mean a vastly different thing than seed-planting as man is aware of in his time/space dimension. In God's dimension, there is no time in which to measure slow growth from a seed to a sprout to full flower. God did not create Adam after His Seed and image as a baby. He created Adam whole and mature in His sight.

As the ages of Christendom move toward the stature of the fullness of Christ, seeds will be sown and growth accelerated to such a degree that the immaturity of yesterday will disappear as a forgotten shade before the brightness of the maturity of the present age. As surely as a nation can be born in a day (Isa. 66:8), so will the Seed of God flower in maturity before our very eyes. The righteousness of God will cover, cleanse, and transform, until His nature is born and increasing in all in the very same miraculous, multitudinous, explosive growth.

GROWTH AND INCREASE OF THE NATURE OF GOD

The expansion and increase, the multiplication of our God will not refer, then, simply to a multiplication of numbers, but it will refer to the expansion of the nature of our God. It will refer to the abounding, exact re-creation of His infinite creativity and wisdom and variety and joy, over and over.

We know that Jesus our Lord fed the multitudes on that long-ago mountain with the multiplication of loaves and fishes—natural food they could recognize, ordinary food used every day. With their own eyes they saw multiplication of bread and fish. And so in these last days man will see the multiplication of ordinary things, things he has always held in his hands as part of the tools of the survival of everyday life. But he will bless it with the blessing of his God, and see it multiplied unto thousands. And all of the wiles of the desperate wicked will come into play, like hailstones. But the righteous in complete calm and confidence will simply bless that small remnant untouched by the wicked, and it will multiply, it will grow and expand, ever-increasing, ever-enlarging.

Thus man will realize that what he has seen in the multiplication of ordinary things has not just been the increase of numbers itself, but the increase of the ability of the dunamis power of Almighty God. Once again, releasing Himself without measure through His earthen vessels, sending out the Word of power with the ability to reproduce itself, over and over, in all the creative force of the One Who originally sent it out. (2 Cor. 9:10)

The Word of God will enlarge, expand, and grow like bread rising from the yeast, when warmth touches it, man releasing it to the corners of the earth (Acts 12:24). Revelation will grow and expand as the mind of man accepts and activates the mind of Christ and stretches to contain the knowledge of his God. For in this time of perpetual light, ever-increasing and perpetual light, man will see old truths with a newness of life, with an expanded revelation. Even as the law was fulfilled in Christ and expanded and illuminated with His light, but not annulled or cast away, so will man receive a revelation of giving, a revelation of the nature of God in His infinite love, creativity and wisdom.

> That their hearts may be encouraged, having been knit together in love, and attaining to all the wealth that comes from the full assurance of understanding, resulting in a true knowledge of God's mystery, that is, Christ Himself, in whom are hidden all the treasures of wisdom and knowledge. Col. 2:2-3

As man continues to unreservedly and unashamedly pour out of the living waters that are within him, showering the earth with the radiance of the glory of the Father of Lights, the spirit of wisdom and understanding will burst upon the horizon like fresh oil, fragrant and spicy. Man will begin to grasp that he has left behind the age of innocence and the age of the knowledge of evil, and has come into another place, a time, a realm, an eternity of righteousness. Expansion, multiplication, increase, and giving will flow out of him as the waters over a dam. All will flow out of him as the rain falls from the heavens, as the steam rises from the warm and well-watered earth; pouring out of him as the fire crackles and burns lustily in the great bonfires of life, thrust out of him like a rocket on a launching pad when the fires propel it into the heavens.

GIVING: A CIRCULAR LIFE-FLOW

This principle of God's multiplication, the pouring out of great increase, springs from a giving heart. In the innermost fountains of the heart of the Father is a wellspring of giving. It is a wellspring that gives without thought of reward. He simply pours out Himself upon the earth that He has made, reproducing all that He is from earthen vessels. As the Body of Christ pours out of the life of God that is within, giving without premeditation, that very power and energy which multiplies itself is released.

The word giving will no longer mean "I take what I have and with an act of my will, I hand it to you, thus meaning that I have a hole left from whence I took it." But giving will be without thought, and there will be no lack. There will be no holes; there will be a life-flow. The Father pours, the earth receives and pours back, seeding the heavens; the heavens pour and the earth receives and pours back; it is a continual cycle, a continual life-flow of giving.

The earth's flow of life-giving water is completely solar-driven. Without the sun the life-flow would cease immediately. The sun causes the difference in temperature which moves the clouds to release the rain. The revolution of the earth on its axis around the sun delineates the seasons of the year which control the flow of rivers and waters. It is the sun that transforms the water into vapor and causes the wind to blow vapors in from the sea. The warmth of the sun causes vapors to rise which seed the clouds with moisture, activating the flow all over again. Multiplication, growth, and increase all are integrally a life-flow of the nature and essence of the life of God, the great Light Who made all. We release His life, freely given to us, and watch it multiply itself, as it seeds the earth unto harvest, producing crops which pour back to Him so that the cycle can continue on its fruitful, joyous path.

Man will open the windows of heaven within him, the floodgates that will never be shut, and he will pour. And pour, and pour, and pour, and pour. And the thirsty earth in this end-time harvest shall greedily receive and receive and receive. And as it receives, it will be instantly transformed by the glory of the Lord into yet another light-giver, another light-bearer, the candle of man lighting another candle and another candle, then another candle. God is raising up laborers, shafts of His great light, ever-increasing, ever-growing, ever-expanding, ever-multiplying their fruitfulness from this world into the next and into the next and into the next, an eternal ever-expanding, ever-growing, ever-glowing, shining and radiant Garden of Great Glory.

X

HARVEST—RESTORATION OF THE GARDEN OF GOD

You are a fountain springing up in a garden, a well of living waters, and flowing streams from Lebanon. Song 4:15 AMP

Central thought: In the time of harvest there will be sounds of the music of heaven manifested on the earth. Singers will sing and prophesy new melodies and harmonies and speak sharp living words; the instruments will prophesy, the harps will play, the drums will crash with heaven's rhythms and the very air will vibrate with the colors and the joys of the music and the sounds around the throne. Vibrations of the power of heaven are arising and shaking, just as the mountains tremble at His presence.

HARVEST—RESTORATION OF THE GARDEN OF GOD

Have you ever been in a hotel or large building on your way to a party, and as you walked down the hall, you could hear the sounds of merrymaking emanating from the room to which you were going? The closer you came to the room, the louder the sounds. At first it was just a cacophony of jumbled noises, but the closer you approached, individual sounds began to emerge: the trill of a woman's laughter, the clink of glasses as refreshing liquids were poured, the ring of silverware as feasting progressed, the sounds of music, movement and life. The closer you came to the sound, the greater the anticipation. You could almost feel the joy and fellowship being exchanged in the room before arrival. And stepping across the threshold as the event itself enveloped you and you became one with it, suddenly you were absorbed and saturated with a totally different perspective and other senses and activities claimed the attention. Anticipation can be almost as exciting as the fulfillment of that which is anticipated.

SOUNDS OF HARVEST

For thus the Lord has told me, "I will look from My dwelling place quietly like dazzling heat in the sunshine, like a cloud of dew in the heat of harvest." Isa. 18:4

"Do you not say, 'There are yet four months, and then comes the harvest'? Behold, I say to you, lift up your eyes, and look on the fields, that they are white for harvest. John 4:35

And another angel came out of the temple, crying out with a loud voice to Him who sat on the cloud, "Put in your sickle and reap, because the hour to reap has come, because the harvest of the earth is ripe." Rev. 14:15

We are approaching the eminent appearing of the door through which we will pass into the greatest harvest that the world has ever seen. The world today is full of anticipation, and the sounds of the great harvest are making themselves heard; far away and dull sounds at first. But they are coming closer and closer, and we are beginning to hear individual sounds rising above the others.

Like Elijah and his servant when the cloud the size of the man's hand was upon the horizon, there is the sound of the abundance of rain. Many can even sniff and smell that indescribable refreshing fragrance of rain in the air. The unprecedented rains that precede harvest, that freshen and spur on final growth, are upon the earth. We have seen restoration of the pastor, the evangelist, the teacher, and even the prophet, but now as the final finger on that mighty hand appears, the apostle joins in the cloud, and the cloud moves steadily on toward the fields. We batten down the hatches and ready ourselves for the storms of life-giving substance.

With the sound of the abundance of rain, one also can hear the sound of the voice of the Lord God walking in the cool of the day (Gen.3:8). For it is the breaking of a new day; the dawn of a new day is upon the horizon. And in the coolness of this time, just as the Lord God walked in the first garden, so His voice walks today across the face of the earth refreshing those who are hungry for His presence. The sound of the Lord God walks in the coolness of the dawn of the breaking of a new day and speaks to His beloved of the vineyards, the fields and the great harvest to come. His voice walks and moves in the breath of the sons of day.

We are sons of the day, we are sons of the light (1 Thes. 5:5), and as the day breaks and the shadows flee away, the sons of God are moving into the fullness of the light of God. The breath that first blew life into Adam now blows across the face of the earth, yes even the sounds of a mighty rushing wind (Acts 2:2). Winds are gusting across the earth, sweeping in the fire of God, blowing out the Seed of God to the four corners of the earth, refreshing the earth and spreading the fragrance of our God to His beloved.

Through the cacophony of the sounds that are arising upon the face of the earth, one can hear the calls of the workers in the vineyard, the shouts of the laborers as they answer God's call to the nations. The sounds of the laborers and their laughter and joy emanates as they rush to the fields. The sounds of the voices of the multitudes rise in a roar as they respond to the trumpet call, to the clarion call of God's sounding throughout the earth. The music of the bride and the bridegroom fills the air as they call and answer one another in the low murmur of love-talk, on the way to the vineyards (Song 7:12).

Over and above all resounds music and singing, with new sounds rising. In the time of harvest there will be the sounds of the music of heaven manifested on the earth, new sounds in the instruments, some seeming strange because they were not made for human ears but outside our time and space dimension. Singers will sing and prophesy new melodies and harmonies and speak sharp living words. The instruments will prophesy, the harps will play, the drums will crash with heaven's rhythms and the very air will vibrate with the colors and the joys of the music and the sounds around the throne. Vibrations of the power of heaven are arising and shaking, just as the mountains tremble at His presence.

Recently I was teaching on the sounds of heaven. As we began to release new sounds and vibrations across the congregation, even the walls seemed to vibrate with the power of heaven. Afterward, a young man came to me, shaking from head to toe, and trying to speak. He said "I am a sound professional... I have to talk to you... I am just vibrating; I am just vibrating." As I left the building he was still standing, shaking and vibrating with the sounds and power of heaven.

So we are in a new place, a new season, an exciting season of harvest. Underneath the froth and fullness of the treble and bass of all of those sounds will be the steady ongoing, grating sound of the millstones grinding grain for the bread for the nations. Amidst the joy and singing, the work of harvest continues and restoration is at hand. All the things taken away in the time of Israel's desolation will be restored to shine in the lamp of the Lamb (Jer. 25:10). God is the orchestrator of the greatest party the world has ever known, and He has been planning it since the worlds began. Now as He lifts His baton, a hush falls, and the music of the ages is heard across the land.

PARABLE OF THE MUSIC OF HARVEST

A minister friend, Debbie Anthony, shared with me an amazing vision that the Lord gave her of the releasing of this amazing music of harvest:

"I saw sheets of white paper with musical notes scattered, thrown upon paper, in a very random fashion. Each musical note was of a unique color or hue, none were black. I saw One Who I knew to be the Master Musician with papers spread before Him on a work table—an arrangement like a drafting table. I saw that the musical notes were alive as the Master Musician began to place staff lines on the pages for the placement of the notes. I saw Him place treble and bass clefs in the proper positions, and I knew that this work brought Him great joy; He seemed to work not in a hurried fashion but with great anticipation.

After He had readied the paper, He began to speak to each note and I knew that He was telling each one where to position itself in this piece of music, which was to be a symphony. It was a very intimate, individual thing as He communicated with each living note. I wondered why He didn't speak just once and command all to take their place; wouldn't that be much more efficient? He knew my question, of course, before I asked it; I knew the answer, too. Still with a joyous smile on His face and somehow without stopping His work, He answered me.

Each one is a precious treasure worthy of His intimate attention, worthy to be adored as they are His creation. So it was with adoration and joy that He continued to speak. I could not hear the individual assignments of each, I only saw notes begin to take their place: here, there, one in the middle, one at the end, one three spaces away from the first. I knew that only a divine musician could write in such a fashion because He already knew the beginning, the middle and the end. I knew that that which would seem to me to be confusion was His perfect plan.

I saw some notes refuse their assignment; they moved off the pages, across His work surface and began to fall. I saw that He, without stopping what He was doing, somehow noticed each one, caught it with His hand and placed it with great care in the bosom of His garment. He seemed to say without saying it, He would attend to them, and also, they had not been lost. I knew that none would be lost that were truly His. I watched as He finished the task and then began to place dynamic markings on the piece and rests in the proper places. With a flourish He placed the double bar at the end of the piece that signifies it is finished!

Then He did a most unusual thing, or at least it was to me until I understood. He pulled from the midst of His being a stringed instrument. He saw my wonderment and somehow without words He asked me the question, "Surely you knew that I and music are one? I am made of that and much more!" When He communicated to me, it was with such joy and loving amusement that He had surprised me again! He seemed to say, "Keep watching!!"

As He began to play the stringed instrument, notes flew from His fingers and from His mouth; He had created this lovely perfect symphony for Himself! I saw the notes fly off into the atmosphere, each unique hue blending with another until they moved with such incredible speed that they formed only blindingly pure white light. And the light had life; it moved; it ran; it pushed; it was a juggernaut in the earth. As it flew, everywhere it went the darkness fled. The darkness ran screaming before it searching for a place to hide. The light was the glory of the Lord covering the earth, and heaven heard the tumult and joined its voices to cry,

'Lift up your heads, O ye gates!
And be ye lifted up ye everlasting doors!
For the King of Glory shall come in!'

The light rushed like water; it blew like the wind; it went where it was destined to go unhindered, unfettered by the pitiful darkness that fled in terror before this wind, this water, this perfect light. I saw that it joined with the heavenly voices of light and flew at an incalculable rate into the vastness of the eternal universe crying as it went: 'Holiness unto the Lord! Holiness unto the Lord!'

And as it went I saw the Great Singer, this Perfect Musician laughing, fulfilled in His creation. I saw that He had known as He spoke to each note what its destiny would be, so that He was not concerned about the discomfort that some had as they waited for others to take their place or the pain that some experienced as they realized the magnitude of the assignment and compared it to their own ability. He knew! I realized that He knew all along! He communicated to me that nothing stirs up His joy any more than His creation hearing His voice, obeying and thus achieving the highest and the best for which they were created. I realized that obeying His voice catapults us into our perfect eternal destiny.

He was exuberant! He literally could not contain Himself! He whirled and leaped expressing the joy that was His. Then He looked at me and I knew that He had enjoyed Himself to such a great extent that He turned to do the same thing—with a new group of notes and another sheaf of paper."

POWER OF HARVEST

> And they sang the song of Moses the bondservant of God and the song of the Lamb, saying, "Great and marvelous are Thy works, O Lord God, the Almighty; righteous and true are Thy ways, Thou King of the nations." Rev. 15:3

A great multitude stretching out like a sea, from every nation and every tribe and every kindred and every clime, a multitude of every sex and every color, a multitude washed from the stains of financial security, physical prowess, having been washed from the stains of athletic ability, and mental gymnastics, having been washed from the stains of the need to excel, the need to fulfill desires and ambitions, a multitude washed from the filth of tradition—this people will have no kinship to anything but the wonder of the Lamb (1 Cor. 2:4). For multitudes are coming, caught in the harvest net, multitudes that no man can number and no man can tame. No man will be able to control or marshal these particular troops, and they will be filled with the praises of a King only recently known. Washed in the blood of the Lamb, they will be clothed in raiment that they do not understand. But the relief of having come from where they were will soothe any lingering questions, and they will relinquish all need to explain, before the joy of the song.

For in this multitude without number, the power of God will march forth in an explosion of light, grace, and mercy such as the world has never known. And power will manifest itself in ways that man has never thought of, and therefore certainly could never orchestrate. The power of God will sing through the air transcending the molecules and the flimsy makeup of what was once a "triumphant" fallen earth. This is seeing the Kingdom of God in full manifestation!

The power of God will transcend and transform until this explosion of light has illumined every blade of grass and every leaf, until the trees of the field clap their hands with revelation of the knowledge of the Lord and the Word of God. The mountains will melt at the Presence of the King, and nature will rejoice, having shed the cries and the agony of birth pangs and travail for the garments of praise and rejoicing at the manifestation of the sons of God (Rom. 8:19).

ACTIVITIES OF HARVEST

In this time of the restoration of all things, man will no longer make his living by the sweat of his brow. The dominion given to Adam will be restored and man will once again have dominion and authority over the crops of the fields, the fowl of the air, the rains and the winds and the waves and storms. And even as the hundred-fold return manifests in the natural, it will manifest in the spiritual, because the natural and the spiritual are becoming one. As the great plowmen of God pour their lives into the harvest of men's souls, the seasons will overlap, and they will continue to plow and plant and grow and harvest (Isa. 37:30).

As there was a time to pluck up and a time to plant, a time to dance and a time to weep and a time to mourn, so this third day, this full day, is the time come full circle for man to rejoice in the work of his God. For time as the husbandmen have known it will have passed away with the night and the shadows of the time/space dimension of mortality.

Life will come out of death, and the waters that flow from the great plowmen, harvesters, waterers and planters as they labor in the vineyards and the fields of the world, pouring out that which is within them, will heal all that they touch (Ez.47:8-12). Angels will walk the fields with the laborers, helping pull in the nets of the great harvest. And many who have longed to see the faces of angels will laugh and walk with them, grateful for their strength and help, for the nets will be heavy (Matt. 13:39, Rev. 14:15, Heb. 12:22).

The laborers sent into this great endeavor will labor under the power and the strength of Almighty God. They will be laborers who have ceased from their own labors and entered into the Sabbath Rest of their God. (Ex. 34:21). But this will not be a rest like any other that man has known. It will not be a rest of leisure where there are no activities. It will be the rest of the flesh, the rest of the soul man, the carnal man, the old man. It will be a retiring of the old wineskins. It will be the putting away of all striving and straining, pushing and pulling, all grunting to bring forth (Heb. 4:1-11).

168

The hundred-fold harvest, the restoration of a fruitful garden full of all manner of pleasant fruit, that restoration will come about through no effort of man. It will come through no plan, program, activity, strategy, or form that man can devise, but God the Father will orchestrate, and His light and His life will be the only light. Natural light will pass away; natural illumination will pass away; natural activity will pass away. Man will move joyously at long last into a realm and a walk by the Spirit, where he is doing just that: walking by the spirit and not by the flesh. Working by the spirit, and not by the flesh. No more sweat. As a priest of the Most High God, in pure linen, he will join the multitudes that sing the song of Moses: "Great and marvelous are Thy works, O Lord God," for they are THY works, and not the works of man.

RELATIONSHIPS OF HARVEST

In this new order of things, relationships will burst forth on new levels. Unity will be a thing long sought after, long desired, and finally attained. For the laborers in this great day of harvest will move as one, in one accord, together, no longer separated by distrust, skepticism, fear, suspicion, doubt, or competition. The walls that have separated the Body of Christ will fall by the wayside, just like the walls of Jericho, as the laborers march to the fields as one, obeying the trumpet call of their God. Doctrine will be unimportant, church statues set up in past centuries by men of great zeal will be unnoticed before the power of the love of God, which will bind with cords that cannot be broken. Laborers in the field will move together, one planting, one watering, one bringing in the grain, hardly noticing whose function is what before the joy of moving in union with the Lord of the Harvest (Luke 10:2).

And when work in the field is done for a time, relationships will continue in the House, as the Body of Christ comes together in greater and greater multitude to celebrate their King. Authority will be a new word with a new meaning. For in the House of the Lord, the authority of God will reign unquestioned, untarnished, and pure. All the tenets and statutes of the faith, having come into sharp focus, will reign unquestioned in every temple of God. And the churches and the temples of the Most High God will run like well-oiled machines, the will of man having finally submitted to the will of God.

The will of man will no longer try to control and rule every portion of the church. The unity of the brethren, having produced the anointing that breaks the yoke, will release that anointing into every area of government and every department of the churches of the world. The anointing that breaks the yoke will do just that: it will break the yokes off of God's people as they come together to worship and continue in the House, the Church, the work of the harvest.

Churches will have to stretch to accommodate the massive ingathering. Facilitating such a massive ingathering would have no longer been possible in the existing structure, turmoil and strife of the wrestling that has gone on in God's churches for centuries. Man wrestling with man over the things of God. In this great day of the Lord, strife will cease. The union of the laborers of the field and the union of the members in the House will be a reflection of the union in the bridal chamber between every believer and his Lord. Man will come into a relationship with his God never before thought or dreamed of. He will live throughout his perpetual day consumed through with the Presence of his God as a prism is a carrier of the laser shafts of rainbow light.

In this season of continual harvest, as the plowman overtakes the reaper, the seasons overlap: plowing, planting, growing, and harvest. The soil stays continually plowed, water is in abundant supply, nature is no longer stingy, temperamental and cruel, and the continual Presence of the Sun becomes the comfort of the skies. The curse has been removed and paradise restored. Jesus said, "Today shalt thou be with Me in paradise." He was speaking of THE DAY. The sons of the day. THIS DAY we will live in His sight, in His paradise. The trees of the fields shall clap their hands and the hills run with honey and milk; the mountains will leap for joy as His will is done in earth as it is in Heaven.

Fear, death, tears, sorrow and sighing will be replaced with expectancy, peace, fulfillment and joy. There will be no fear of harsh elements and adverse circumstances. There will be no fear of limited seed. There will be no fear of sickness and inability to work. There will be no fear of plagues and pestilence. For harvest will be for the purpose of sowing again and life more abundant. The most important part of the harvest will be the part faithfully replanted. For harvest and heaven, paradise and millennial reign will not be filled with idle and aimless endeavor. Harvest will not be a one-time blessing, but a continual cycle of life. And as the sounds, the music, the power, the activities and the relationships of harvest begin to manifest, man will live in a perpetual rainbow of the sign of God's covenant. The fulfillment of God's promises. The manifestation of God's joy. "Thou shalt multiply the nation, Thou shalt increase their gladness; they will be glad in Thy presence as with the gladness of harvest, as men rejoice when they divide the spoil" (Isa. 9:3).

The time of harvest will be filled with the feastings of our God as He lays the table for His beloved. "He has brought me to his banquet hall, and his banner over me is love" (Song 2:4). Harvesters will not only bring in the crops, but they will eat of the fruit of the vine with the Lord of the Harvest in His eternal, everlasting Kingdom.

CONCLUSION

And We Shall Live in His Sight

And we shall live in His sight. Then shall we know, if we follow on to know the Lord: His going forth is prepared as the morning; and He shall come unto us as the rain, as the latter and former rain unto the earth. Hosea 6:2c-3, KJV

Harvest begins in the human heart. Restoration of the garden begins in the human heart, wherein lies the garden of God. All of the elements of propagation: seed, soil, plowing, rain, light, growth—all are found within the ultimate creation of the Most High God, the heart of man. The divine Seed placed within that earthen vessel contains within it the new heaven and the new earth. In it lies the explosive power and joy of the time of harvest. All of the tortuous, laborious ages have culminated, unfolded, led and progressed into one simple and common destiny, that is the restoration of the human spirit into unity with the heart of the Father. All the songs ever sung, all the tears ever shed, all the cries ever heard, all the races ever run, all the music ever written points to one small and seemingly insignificant and unseen entity: the heart of man.

God created the heart and spirit of man in His own image. But that heart became a wayward heart, choosing knowledge, the enticing words of man's wisdom over the Spirit and Presence of Him Who made it all, choosing to walk through the fields of rebellion and lost-ness. But God has restored the breach through Christ. God is repairing and raising up. And what God restores, in the pouring out of His giving and fruitful nature, He will make much more full and complete than it ever was before.

PREPARE

As we prepare for the greatest outpouring of the Spirit of God that man has ever known, seen or dreamed of, let us earnestly consider the garden within our own heart.

Let us consider the frailty of our flesh, the weakness of our will, and the fallibility of our emotions.

Let us, with the apostle Paul, crucify the flesh that would so exalt itself above the knowledge of God.

Let us decrease that He may increase on the inside of us.

Let us so step into the life-flow of Almighty God, that the grave clothes and the ragged skins of our old nature and our past fall by the wayside as we race with Him upon the wings of the winds into other galaxies, other worlds and other realms. Not in mind over matter, but hidden in the all-inclusive, the all-encompassing Nature of Him Who makes a way in the wilderness and releases rivers in the desert.

Let us cleave only to Him Who comes to take the wayward, carnal soul and the adamant, rebellious, self-centered body, and transform it by His power truly and totally into one of His children, into thus being part of Himself, one with Him for all eternity, His well-watered garden, and His great delight.

PRAYER FOR HARVEST

Dear Father,

O Thou who gave thought to our forms before there was as yet a breath or a ray of light...

O Thou mighty One who shines in a hidden and mysterious place brighter by millions of years than the sun...

O Thou Who flung the stars in space and hung galaxies without number according to Thy eternal and perfect sight...

O Thou greatest One of all the great Who knew these words before ever one trembled in our being...

O Thou our song and our life Who gives light to our eyes and breath to our lips and Who loves with love so vast and unknowable that the mind of man can only sigh and wonder and wait...

O Thou our life our joy and our all, allow these poor mortals to bring their trembling selves before You with one petition: Let us know you! Not that we ourselves could ever dare to such an elevation, but by the petition and intercession and sacrifice of Your Son Jesus, Who gave us the hope of glory.

Conclusion

We ask that You invade this quivering flesh, these poor shells of mortality, that You pervade these miserable minds that ever strive and fight and cry; that You manifest Your power throughout all the flimsy fibers of our being: blow all the circuits, throw all the breakers, no matter the cost or the consequence, though we die in the process—we entreat You to end this unendurable, unfulfilled longing and satisfy and silence it with Yourself. In Your infinite and vast wisdom, please impart new sight to our eyes, that the gaze of mortality become the brightness of a new day. Blow upon these pitiful ashes and consume the scales over our eyes and the calluses over our hearts and transform us that we might sustain union with the One Who gave first thought and then word to our lives.

Take us in. Keep us ever.

Hold us closer than thought, nearer than breath and dearer and more intimate than any mere earthly embrace.

Consume us with Yourself until there is none left but You: an ever-shining, out-raying of the divine nature of the One Who fills all the universes with the glory of Himself. Amen.

APPENDIX

Cover Art

"The Jeweled Hills" acrylic painting by Erin Hanson

PROPHETIC SIGNIFICANCE: Restoration of the Garden of the Lord

She replied, My beloved has gone down to his garden, to the beds of spices, to feed in the gardens and to gather lilies. Song of Solomon 6:2 AMPC

A fountain of gardens, a well of living waters, and streams from Lebanon. Awake, O north wind, and come, O south! Blow upon my garden, that its spices may flow out. Let my beloved come to his garden and eat its pleasant fruits. Song of Solomon 4:15-16 NKJV

The LORD will guide you continually, and satisfy your soul in drought, and strengthen your bones; you shall be like a watered garden, and like a spring of water, whose waters do not fail. Isaiah 58:11 NKJV

In this season of continual harvest, as the plowman overtakes the reaper, the seasons overlap: plowing, planting, growing, and harvest. The soil stays continually plowed, water is in abundant supply, nature is no longer stingy, temperamental and cruel, and the continual Presence of the Sun becomes the comfort of the skies. The curse has been removed and paradise restored. Jesus said, "Today shalt thou be with Me in paradise." He was speaking of THE DAY. The sons of the day. THIS DAY we will live in His sight, in His paradise. The trees of the fields shall clap their hands and the hills run with honey and milk; the mountains will leap for joy as His will is done in earth as it is in Heaven. (Chapter 10)

FRONT INSIDE COVER BANNER PHOTO

For the earth shall be filled with the knowledge of the glory of the lord as the waters cover the sea. Habb. 2:14

PROPHETIC SIGNIFICANCE OF THE BANNER: The whirlwind in Ezekiel chapter one came from the north, bringing the glory of the Lord. In this banner, the silver whirlwind (representing redemption of the whole man) swirls around, into, and out of a golden runner, running the race set before him toward the prize of the high call of God in Christ Jesus (Phil. 3:14). He is arrayed in golden light, much as the sun coming as a bridegroom out of his chamber (Ps. 19).

In the midst of the runner, the "world" represents this new creation (2 Cor. 5:17) as the new earth, and also indicates the worldwide harvest of the endtime laborer. The whirlwind cascades from the runner into waters, much as natural winds often bring rain. As each of the many-membered Body releases the living water from within (John 7:38), spreading His light and glory throughout the nations, truly the "voice of many waters" (Ez. 43:2) will cover the earth as the waters cover the sea. "Life will come out of death, and the waters that flow from the great plowmen, harvesters, waterers and planters as they labor in the vineyards and the fields of the world, pouring out that which is within them, will heal all that they touch." (Chapter 10)

The runner holds the scroll of the Word of the Lord in his right hand, running in the stead of Christ as part of the end-time army (Joel 2). The mighty right hand of the Captain of the Lord's hosts is full of victory, and His Word runs to the ends of the earth accomplishing His purposes. All of us run our part in the great purpose and plan of the Most High, passing the baton in the fullness of time, one planting, one watering, and another bringing in the harvest.

Each word visually depicts its meaning through its distinctive color and design.

"For the Earth" is reddish-brown, the color of the dust into which God blew His Breath.

"Shall Be" is full of rainbow colors edged with gold speaking of God's covenant with man, and His deity, ours through adoption as His sons (Eph. 1:5).

"Filled" is blue (divine revelation), and is covered with beaded and sequined flowers showing that, fulfilled in the revelation of His glory, we are the garden of the Lord (S.S. 6:2) jeweled as a bride adorned for her husband (Rev. 21:2).

"With the Knowledge" is iridescent white, for the "wisdom that cometh down from above is pure, peaceable, and gentle" (James 3:17). The splendor of the knowledge of His glory shines with all the colors in the spectrum of light. "Of the Glory" is iridescent gold, speaking of divine nature, radiance, majesty, and power (Hab. 3:4).

"Of the Lord" in red reminds us of His saving redemptive blood and His consuming fire that refines and purifies pure gold.

"As the Waters Cover the Sea" shimmer in blues and greens speaking of divine revelation, hope, and the eternal, everlasting Father.

The shining Word of the Lord is portrayed in this banner on a background of black velvet, signifying that He has brought us out of darkness into the marvelous and splendid Light of the knowledge of His Great Glory.

BACK INSIDE COVER BANNER PHOTO

"And we will live in his sight."

After two days He will revive us: in the third day He will raise us up, and we will live in His sight. Then shall we know, if we follow on to know the Lord: His going forth is prepared as the morning; and He shall come unto us as the rain, as the latter and former rain unto the earth. Hosea 6:2-3

PROPHETIC SIGNIFICANCE OF THE BANNER: Circles speak of the unbroken, eternal nature of covenant. In this banner, the circle of the earth and the glowing rainbow speak of the joy of fulfilled covenant. The bejeweled and verdant blue and green earth signifies the fruitfulness of undreamed-of harvest and never-ending supply. A river of life (green for life and hope) pours and tumbles out of the word "live", speaking of the refreshing waters of resurrection life flowing freely from every believer. Redeemed, glorified saints with hands raised in praise and triumph circle the globe, feet firmly planted on earth, as they (like the first-born, Jesus) have overcome the kingdoms of this world. Their hands are joined to indicate the unity of the brethren in the last days. The waters tumble over the people, some to the ankle and some the knee and the waist. Others are inundated by the tumultuous living waters. The entire banner joyously proclaims the fullness and fruitfulness of our face-to-face relationship with the King of Glory, and the glorious beauty of the restored Garden of God.

BOOKS & RESOURCES

LORA ALLISON AND CELEBRATION INTERNATIONAL MINISTRIES

KINGDOM ALIGNMENT, AN ILLUMINATION OF THE KING

Kingdom Alignment opens our hearts to see and understand in a realm that few understand today. Written with prophetic insight and an artist's dramatic flair, this book urges us on to true Kingdom life, devoid of pretense and filled with adventure. God's Kingdom is the only place to dwell if we are to achieve our divine purpose. Prepare your heart for the journey found in this warm and wonderful book as we learn to align ourselves with the Kingdom of God and with our King.

STRESS RELIEF: REFLECTIONS FOR SATURDAY MORNINGS

This is a devotional book designed to be read in those wonderful mornings with the Lord. It contains real life stories of pleasure, treasure, and testing, and will bring refreshing and strength for the week ahead.

FLAMING PURPOSE

Lora Allison's story is filled with fires, floods, and mighty testimonies of the delivering and healing power of our risen Savior. Written in a readably warm and humorous style, this book also contains teaching on the powerful subject of fire.

OVERCOMER: THE EMERGING CHURCH OF THE THIRD DAY

A devotional find, prophetic words to the Body of Christ encourage and strengthen us. Teaching with a fresh perspective enlightens hungry hearts who long for God's eternal Light, Truth, and Holiness.

CELEBRATION: BANNERS, DANCE AND HOLINESS IN WORSHIP

A scriptural look at worship in the beauty of holiness, with insight both visionary and practical involving banners and dance, with how-to's, diagrams, and 59 glorious color photographs. Gift-book quality.

CONVIVIUM PROPHETIC WORSHIP DVD

This glorious video consists of worship clips taken from Celebration conferences held in Houston, Texas. Enjoy the colorful prophetic music, dance, and movement of flags and banners and bask in the powerful anointing of the Holy Spirit. Great for times of personal devotion.

SCHOOL OF PROPHETIC MINISTRY: RELEASING THE RIVER WITH WISDOM

17 Hours of teaching, Flash Drive
Prophetic classes with Celebration Ministries are designed to be informative, enjoyable, and practical. Releasing the River with Wisdom consists of two intensive series of courses and are designed to provide Biblically based instruction concerning the gifts of the Spirit, and an encouraging and safe atmosphere for them to develop. Our purpose is to study together God's Word with an emphasis toward prophecy and prophetic ministers, protocol and order, working in the Kingdom, as well as submission to and in New Testament local church authority.

FIRESTORM PROPHETIC WORSHIP: PREPARING TO RUN

Spontaneous Prophetic Worship Recorded Live: Unusual sounds and music accompany prophetic worship as heavenly sounds flow through the powerful anointing released by gifted singers and musicians. 2 CD Music Set.

THE SUPERNATURAL LIFE: LIVING IN THE SLIPSTREAM OF HEAVEN

We must learn to slip into heaven's mass, heaven's atmosphere of power, the stream of heaven's winds and out of earth's pull and atmosphere, the carnal life, and reside in the SLIPSTREAM OF HEAVEN. True union with Him in Spirit is LIVING THE SUPERNATURAL LIFE! 10 Hour Video Teaching Series.

www.celebrationministries.com
Books Available E-Book, www.amazon.com

CPSIA information can be obtained
at www.ICGtesting.com
Printed in the USA
BVHW011148021019
560025BV00006B/54/P